DADAMONI

DADAMONI

The Life and Times of Ashok Kumar

NABENDU GHOSH

Foreword by
BHARTI JAFFREY

Afterword by
RATNOTTAMA SENGUPTA

SPEAKING TIGER PUBLISHING PVT. LTD
125A, Ground Floor, Shahpur Jat,
Near Asiad Village, New Delhi 110049

First published in hardback by HarperCollins Publishers India in 1995

This revised edition published by Speaking Tiger in paperback in 2022

Copyright © Ratnottama Sengupta 2022
Foreword copyright © Bharti Jaffrey 2022

ISBN: 978-93-5447-205-3
eISBN: 978-93-5447-197-1

10 9 8 7 6 5 4 3 2 1

The moral right of the author has been asserted.

All rights reserved.

No part of this publication may be reproduced,
transmitted, or stored in a retrieval system, in any form or
by any means, electronic, mechanical, photocopying,
recording or otherwise, without the prior
permission of the publisher.

This book is sold subject to the condition that it shall not,
by way of trade or otherwise, be lent, resold, hired out,
or otherwise circulated, without the publisher's
prior consent, in any form of binding or cover
other than that in which it is published.

Contents

Foreword: My Papa, Ashok Kumar   vii
Preface   xxi

1. Discovery of a Hero   1
2. His Family Tree   5
3. The Actor Who Covered His Face   12
4. Bioscope Was Wonderful   19
5. The Boat of Life   23
6. The Boat of Life Moors   30
7. The Little Actor Uncovers His Face   33
8. Eyes Harbour the Heart   43
9. Kismet   52
10. Playing God   58
11. From a River unto the Sea   71
12. A Man of Many Roles   88
13. An Actor's Role in Cinema   98
14. His Many Many Heroines   110
15. Every Jack Has His Jill   113

Afterword: Bombay Talkies to Bollywood:
The Legend of Dadamoni 124

Filmography 142

Index 182

FOREWORD
My Papa, Ashok Kumar

Papa,

As I sit down to pen these lines, I marvel at the fact that you, my father, were the first superstar of Indian cinema—for seven continuous years Roxy Cinema at Churni Road, Mumbai, showed only Ashok Kumar films. But more importantly, you were one of the pioneers who laid the foundation of what we call Bollywood today. So, it amazes me that you started as a most unwilling, reluctant actor!

To encapsulate sixty-four years of experience and 350 films—an average of six films every year—in a couple of thousand words is a daunting task, but I must try as that alone can give an idea of your achievement to a generation that came into the world after you exited it.

13 October 1911—110 years ago you were born in Bhagalpur and grew up in Khandwa. And like your father and others in his family, you too took to studying law once you completed your BSc in Calcutta. There you came under the spell of movies and decided that five lawyers were enough in one family, so you decided to become a director! But being the sensitive person that you were, you had a vision for films: because it is such a powerful medium, you wanted to educate people even as they were entertained.

With this in mind, you reached Bombay where your brother-in-law Sashadhar Mukherjee was working with Bombay Talkies. Since you wanted to be a director, being a lab assistant seemed the best way to master film-making. Happily, you started learning editing, music and photography. Your progress made Himanshu Rai, the founder of Bombay Talkies, very happy. But when he wanted to cast you as the lead actor of *Jeevan Naiya*, you were terrified. 'I am not an actor and I certainly don't want to be a hero!' you had asserted. You tried your level best to escape—in vain. Eventually you did nine films with Franz Osten, your first director!

There must have been something in you: every one of these was a major hit. And, although you were some way from being perfect, people loved you. They could relate to the awkward young man—and a star was born. You rose to the heights of stardom beyond the imagination of even Uncle Sashadhar and your mentor. So, you tried to better yourself as an actor. But there was no school of acting then, no systematic approach to cultivate the 'art of experiencing' which Konstantin Stanislavky had put in place to train theatre actors in Russia. In the absence of a place to master Method Acting, you did the only thing you could to 'educate' yourself in the art: you started watching Hollywood films. You watched how actors like Humphrey Bogart carried themselves. You read up books on acting. You recognised the weakness in your voice and would go to the seashore to practice voice-throwing. You put in hard work and grit to raise yourself to a certain standard in acting.

Once you attained heights as an actor, you took to producing films. Actually all your life you wanted to be a director—perhaps that explains why you could produce the most popular films of those times: *Mashal*, *Majboor* and *Ziddi*, among others. In *Ziddi*, you introduced a new face, Dev Anand the eternal lover *and* gave a platform to your younger brother Kishore Kumar as singer. The two of them, together and individually, went on to become major senstations of Indian screen. These are just two names, there were scores of others you honed into gems.

~

Was there something in your DNA, Papa, that prompted you to push your boundaries again and again? Every time you scaled a peak you wanted to explore untrod fields. That is how you wrote the story of *Mahal* which brought to cine lovers the beautiful Madhubala and the nightingale Lata Mangeshkar, with the timeless song '*Aayega aanewala…*' It is iconic even today. You had taken a risk with its theme of reincarnation, you did not know if it would work. You gave it to a distributor for only Rs 4 lakh on the condition that he would not see the film until its release. The distributor agreed since you were the biggest star of the times—and sure enough it struck gold. We still love what you had imagined so many moons ago.

For you, a success signalled it was time to move ahead. So you risked the image of a 'hero', a person we look up to and want to emulate, and played a villain. Thus came *Sangram* which, in 1950, ran every day at 3, 6 and 9 p.m. in packed houses for sixteen weeks. One can measure the success of your performance from another fact: in the sixteenth week the police commissioner came home to say that Chief Minister Morarji Desai had decided to ban the film. Why? Because of the impact of your performance!

This film was about a boy who is spoiled by his indulgent father, and gets into nefarious activities: he gambles and kidnaps the girl he loves and takes her hostage. Years later this was to be remade as *Shakti*.

That day you tried to explain to the police commissioner that the film has a moral, that 'the hero gets his punishment.' But he said, 'Dadamoni, the problem is that you are on the other side of the law. In the gun fight when you shoot and the police get injured, the audience was cheering for you! The law cannot permit this.' He added, 'You are a role model, Dadamoni, people want to follow you and will end up against the law. We cannot let you do that.'

You realised that you had glamorised violence. So on second thought, you did some 'boring Inspector roles'. But as was your want, you poured life into these even if they were not central chracters.

You had another realisation: 'In acting, you have to give so much of yourself, yet not be yourself.' Meaning, an actor must draw from his own experiences to *be* somebody else. That is why you were so convincing even in guest appearances. People overlooked the craft in your screen avatars, they believed that you were simply there! Were you peeved by this, Papa? *'Aap toh acting hi nahin kartey!'* they say, you lamented, 'People think it is not difficult to act.' But there is a large measure of thought, preparation and empathy that goes into acting and it is far from easy to make it look effortless and natural. You exemplified this, for you would always drew from within.

~

Your next gamble was *Kanoon*, which was a film on the practice of capital punishment. It brought into debate whether to hang or not to hang? Can the State take a life on the basis of claims by an eyewitness? Should one man's word cost another man his life? A man is depicted as a murderer but later it comes out that he was innocent although there was no evidence to bear him out. Today the capital punishment is given in the 'rarest of rare' cases. Moreover, at least in Delhi High Court, a person whose true identity is unknown or withheld in a legal action is referred to as 'Ashok Kumar'. Papa, the root of this practice lies in your characterisation of Badri Prasad, the judge suspected of being the culprit!

But Papa, you knew that you were doubling the risk, didn't you? Because *Kanoon* was the first Hindi film without a single song. This, at a time when songs were the public expression of every emotion of the characters, particularly of romance! Just imagine risking this in the year of *Mughal-e-Azam, Kohinoor, Anuradha, Chaudhavin Ka Chand* and *Jis Desh Mein Ganga Behti Hai*. All these hits of 1960 had music as a key component and *Kanoon* had none! It required none—such was the compelling power of the courtroom drama. 'Please don't do this,' people advised, 'it's a recipe for disaster!' Most distributors were apprehensive when they came to preview the 'movie that had no song': will the audience accept such an experiment?

I believe B.R. Chopra, keen to know their reaction, was unnerved when silence greeted him. He is said to have offered to insert a couple of songs with the help of music director Salil Chowdhury. But the stunning twist at the end proved the clinching factor. The distributors preferred the 'masterpiece' as it was, and history was made. Clearly, the action was so gripping that viewers too did not want to be disturbed, and *Kanoon* became a milestone.

Its message was, of course, the most absorbing factor of *Kanoon* but then most of your films then had a social conscience. They always passed on a little message. *Ek Hi Raasta* was about widow remarriage, which at that time was frowned upon. If truth be told, our society still does not approve of it. *Meri Soorat Teri Aankhen* was about an ugly man with a lovely voice, in love with a beautiful girl who never knew this adorable voice belonged to such an ugly face. It was the perennial story of inner and outer beauty, of good looks versus good soul. One day I told you, 'Papa, how ugly you are in this film!' You replied, 'You have to decide for yourself: Do you want to be a good actor or do you want to look good all the time?'

At once I understood that you, Papa, wanted to reinvent yourself all the time. And the audience loved you because of this, as much as your smooth, natural style of acting. No swagger, not too much dialogue for you. 'That would be preaching!'—you would protest. So you mastered the art of sub-texting: you would speak your lines, you would say the dialogue but beyond that you would leave a lot unsaid. You perfected the technique to the point where viewers had no difficulty in following what you left unsaid.

Before long they loved you for whatever you did, as villain or comedian. By this time perhaps you had also realised that you cannot be a star all your life. So you concentrated more and more on becoming a character actor. And you created memorable characters like Bikash, the freedom fighter in *Bandini* who promises to marry Kalyani but ends up marrying a hysteria patient whom she murders. Indian cine viewers still debate, 'Why should Nutan go with an ageing and unwell Ashok Kumar when the young and handsome doctor Dharmendra wants to marry her?' But I know, as did you, that Nutan had insisted, 'Dadamoni and Dadamoni alone can be Bikash.' Her trust was borne out by the script, the director and by the silver trophy at Karlovy Vary.

How smoothly you played the dark shades so alien to you Papa! Judge Ajay in *Do Bhai* turned out to be a murderer. Dr Prakash in *Aarti* ruined the marriage of his junior doctor when she breaks their engagement to marry an unemployed youth. The blinded-in-war Major Chandrakant of *Oonchey Log* gives shelter to and protects a fugitive from the police—only to find out that the man has murdered his younger son. Raju is the elder brother of Radha, the orphaned siblings in *Raakhi* who grow up through hardship to end as business rivals. This film not only won you a Filmfare award, it won you a sister for life: every year on rakshabandhan, Waheeda Rehman would tie you this thread of sibling bonding. If ever she forgot, you would call her and demand, 'What day is it today?' Justly so, to date, every year rakshabandhan, every home and street resounds with the song, '*Bandha huwa hai iss dhaage mein bhai behen ka pyaar...*'

All this happened in 1960s. Long before this, with only six months of singing Yaman in your youth, you had charmed an entire generation with your singing. There are many numbers to bear out that your talent was not limited to acting. Let me mention just one: In 1968 Kishore Kaka and Manna Dey did an inimitable comic song, '*Ek chatur naar karke sringar*'. In the film *Padosan*, my uncle himself acted as the playback friend and mentor of the hero, Sunil Dutt, while Manna Dey was the voice of Mehmood. To this day how many people know that it was a remix version of '*Ek chatur naar kar kar shringar*', which you first sang in 1941 for *Jhoola*? There was no playback then. How hard it must have been for you to sing and act the scene that also required you to bathe in cold water! I remember you telling me that when '*Ban ki chidiya*' was recorded for *Achhut Kanya*, musicians sat on another tree with a harmonium, tabla and other musical instruments. At one point the weight of these instruments led to them falling off the tree! Is that why you were so happy when playback singing became the rule?

Today everything has changed in film-making. Technology has made it so easy to record songs in multiple takes, to add the music track separately, or even to shoot a film on digital camera. You did not have any of these luxuries then. So we can scarcely imagine how much hard work went into creating the clime that obtains today. But such was your passion for your work that you never complained, of heat, reflectors, false beards, wigs, anything—unless you were unwell.

~

In 1966 you fell ill with Peritonitis—inflammation of the intestines—and went to America for a serious surgery. On your return, Dev Anand approached you along with Vijay Anand. 'Dadamoni, are you still willing to take risks?' they asked you. 'Will you play the villain again—a jewel thief?' 'But why do you want me to play this role?' you had asked in reply. 'Because you don't look like a jewel thief at all,' the very capable director had answered. 'So there will be an element of surprise for the audience who will never suspect you!' Sure enough, they loved you. For, you played the villain with such aplomb that Dev Anand came to you at the premier and said, 'Dadamoni, you stole the film from me, hanh!'

Then came *Gumraah* on the theme of infidelity. Here you gave your wife the option to choose: Did she want to go back to her lover or stay on with her husband? Half a century ago, it was a big deal to give your wife this choice. And why only then? Don't we read about murder for revenge or honour killings in the papers even today?

Not long after this you graduated to senior roles and smoothly went on to play grandfather—something actors dread as 'the end' of their screen careers. But in your case? People realised that older people too have a life to share with children. That, they can tell wonderful stories because they are free of everyday responsibilities. Soon people started thinking, 'Wow! It might be good to have an older person living in the house!' Today this is a big problem faced by nuclear families.

Around this time, you acted in *Aashirwad* which won you the National Award. And with this film you took another musical stride: You introduced rap, just rhythm and poetry as song. Today we have every gully boy honing the art. *Aashirwad* again was a socially oriented film, this time, about the bond between a father and his daughter. You played a man who broke social rank and made friends with a drummer—and when his friend's daughter is raped, he inadvertently kills the rapist and goes to jail. Years go by before he is released; by then his own daughter has grown up and is getting married.

This is one film that I identified the most with, perhaps because of the persona: you too were such a lively father, telling stories, singing songs. And it is a heart-rending depiction of the father-daughter bond—I have never been able to sit through a second viewing of the film! *Mili* too was a highly emotional story of an agonised father who realises that his daughter is going to die of cancer. But in *Khatta Meetha*, as the Parsi widower with five children who marries a widow with three of her own, you essayed the opposite mood with such aplomb that it created a minor classic! Of course, many of these later films had flaws too but no one could fault your portrayal: you always etched these characters convincingly, without caricaturish flourish.

~

But you immersed yourself in all these characters without any expectation of award or accolade. Except the National Award, the only other award you craved was the appreciation of your viewers. You got the Padma Bhushan, the Dadasaheb Phalke, many a Lifetime Achievement award. Your invariable reaction was, '*Kaun sa sher maar diya hai*? What's the big achievement (in this)?' But your pursuit of excellence was exemplary from the very beginning. I never forgot the singular laurel that had come to you after the release of *Achhut Kanya*. Among the flood of letters and telegrams was one that said 'Congratulations Ashok Kumar on the success of *Achhut Kanya*.' Below it, the signature read 'Adolf Hitler'. 'How could you tear and throw away such an historical document, Papa!' I had cried out. I will never forget your words: 'Laurels can never be more important than principles and human values.' Those were the years when the Nazis were on the rise, you reminded us.

So, more than awards and accolades, you were really happy pursuing your hobbies. Where did you, with only twenty-four hours in a day like any of us, get the time to pursue your hobbies? The full credit here must go to Mummy who took such good care of you, your food, your comfort. She spent her days in the kitchen cooking, but children were not half as important in her life, which revolved around you. However, between 7 and 10 a.m. she did not let anyone disturb you in your bathroom! She herself did not interfere as you sat there and read your dialogue for the day, or painted, or read. Mummy ensured you had your space, to do anything you wanted to. After that you would have your breakfast and leave for work. We knew Papa, that those three hours were very precious to you. Thank god in those days there was no social media—Instagram, Twitter, Facebook. No one had heard of anything other than the telephone which, in any case, would always be answered by Khursheed Mian, your trusted Jeeves and chauffeur for forty-seven years.

Mummy was also the reason why you started doing Homeopathy earnestly. She was very ill—her congenital heart problem had acted up, so you started her on homeopathy. Before long you started doing it as a social service. Your social conscience was so strong that you saw patients on your off days. And did you have a healing touch! All your patients got cured. The biggest success was a fourteen-year-old girl who had developed gangrene. Her leg was to be cut off, which was a shock for her parents and even more, for the girl herself. You sat up for three days and three nights, without a wink of sleep, to find an antidote in Homeopathy and in six months you cured her. It was a major triumph, and to this day Riddhi Hospital in Ghatkopar has a ward named after you.

~

You could have also made a career as a painter, no Papa? Your Grandpa actually wanted to send you to Italy to master the art when you were only twenty. Surely you had it in you: that is why in 1954, while shooting *Bhai Bhai* for AVM in Madras, you took two days off and visited Paul Raj, an artist you had read about in an international magazine on art. And why did you travel some 60 miles away from the city? Because this artist had mastered in the art of painting watercolours without first pencilling the figures. Over two days you learnt to paint in the same manner—I know this because I was with you on that visit. This became your creative outlet when you fell sick and were confined to bed, in 1960s. And, at Iftikhar Uncle's suggestion, you continued to paint even after you recovered. You were so good at it that when M.F. Husain saw your paintings, he said, 'These are not the strokes of an amateur.'

Your mastery over language too was staggering. How many languages did you speak? Eight, or nine? German, French, English, Hindi, Sanskrit, Urdu, Bengali. You taught me a French poem when I was learning French in school. You learnt to write Urdu from Dilip Kumar, and copied your dialogues in Urdu because 'it's like shorthand,' you said. Besides Hindi you acted in Bengali, Marathi and Gujarati films. So it was more than eight! Because, to you, a language was an expression of culture. You believed that the minute you speak a language you bond with the culture and tradition of all these people. Was that why you were so happy when, four days before you passed on, I recited a Persian poem you had taught me as a child?

~

Talking of Dilip Kumar, Papa, was there any co-star you did not got along with? You would, of course, gleefully recount that Raj Kapoor was peeved because, at his wedding, while the nuptials were being ceremonised, his bride, Krishnaji, lifted her veil and stared at you. You were the superstar then! 'You are watching him when I am your groom!'—Rajji had said. And what a handsome bridegroom he was too! Yet men and women, actors, directors, music directors, old or young—every one of them in your time—was happy and proud to be on the sets with you. You had the kind of temperament which comes from the school of thought that believed everything should be shared.

~

On looking back, I realise there was a certain happiness in you which you could spread in the people around you. You were always laughing. Of course, your image was that of a staid old man, but you were full of fun. Even more fun than Kishore Kaka—one only had to see you in your elements! But you always told us, 'There is no happiness outside of yourself, it is always within you. Seek inside, and always, you will find happiness from within you.' This is perhaps the greatest lesson you have taught us, your children.

Being the first born I was fortunate to have known you the longest as a father. And never can I remember you being ostentatious. On the sets your dress had to be perfect, just right for the role. But once you got home, you would dress only in white kurta pajamas. 'Papa, once in a while dress differently!'—I would plead. No, only white kurta pajama after the evening bath, for the terrace gatherings with us children, and Kishore Kaka when he joined in. Those hours were for storytelling—with background score by Kishore Kumar, who perched himself at the piano and played tunes, sometimes sad, sometimes fun!

Even after you reached the zenith of stardom, your life was marked by a simplicity which even I cannot fathom. '*Ghar ki murgi dal barabar*,' you would tease us, 'I'm common, for you see me every day at home.' Yet you opened every door of experience for us. You were so liberal while upbringing us, you told me to watch not just Hindi films but world cinema. 'Go see *Bicycle Thieves* and *Roshomon*...' But you, like your peers, did not want me to do films! Because? 'It would be difficult to marry you off!' you would say. Your unshakeable faith in the values given to you by your upper-middle-class parents stayed with you, and you instilled the same values in your children. Is that why, after I turned twelve, you liked to see me in a sari, at least at home?

The most important of your values was moderation, equilibrium. Whether your films were hits or flops, you never expressed happiness or sorrow. You believed that, for the pursuit of excellence, you have to focus, with truth, integrity and sincerity, in whatever you do, no matter what problems come your way. 'Don't be distracted by the trappings of money, house, car—all that will come but when you lose your focus, you lose all that too.'

Discipline was a big, very big, part of you. You lived your whole life on the belief that without discipline you cannot empower yourself. I can't recall you indulging yourself; you never binged, you always ate 'rationed' food. Maybe that is why you remained so active till the age of eighty-eight. And your homeopathy must have helped too. You hated invasive medicine and hated to be on the respirator when you had to be on one in Jaslok Hospital, because you had difficulty breathing following asthmatic attacks. You had no regret when you passed away at the age of ninety. You always said, 'I have had such a good life, so much adulation from people in every walk of life!'

My youngest sister Preeti—Palu to us—once recalled a day when you had gone to her school and unleashed a flurry as everyone came out to greet you. Palu was then in class IV of St Anne's. That evening she had asked you in awe, 'Papa, do you know everybody in my school?' 'Yes, I know everybody,' you had smiled. You did not tell her that everybody in India knew YOU!

Years later, Palu recounted another lesson she had learnt that day. 'Dad came to pick me up in a big car, either a Buick or a Chevrolet, and that is what had impressed me first. Suddenly it dawned on me that *Dad* had come to take me home! Other children's parents would pick them up after school—mine never came. Now Dad was here! So I started running to him, when girls from the senior classes broke out in amazement: 'Wow! It's Ashok Kumar!' 'THE Ashok Kumar is here!' 'Your father is Ashok Kumar the actor?!'

'At once my carefree and casual gait altered. I started walking with my head in the sky. And just as I was about to reach the car, I stumbled and fell flat on the ground. I felt so small! Somehow, I got up and climbed into the car. Dad was sitting there, an indulgent smile playing on his lips. And he said, "Never keep you head in the clouds, you are apt to stumble over a pebble."'

That day you gave her a mantra for life: Never be so proud that you can't look down. Keep your head on your shoulders and you can walk through life.

~

I really came to appreciate you more as a father when you were no more. Being with you was like being in a workshop. I learnt so much from you! But you never 'taught' us, you never said 'Do this' or 'Don't do that!' You always taught us by exposing us to experiences—and by your fantastic storytelling. You cooked up stories and we listened spellbound. 'Really Papa?!' we would ask but never disbelieve, such was the mesmerising power of your imagination. You never remembered these stories afterwards but one day an elderly gentleman who visited the sets of *Mahal* reminded you, 'When you were five years old, you used to tell me stories about flying tigers...' And who was this gentleman? None other than Sarat Chandra Chatterjee, the king of storytelling whose *Devdas* still enchants the world. In fact, you bought the rights to *Parineeta* as the first film of Ashok Kumar Productions.

Your storytelling, your films, your music—you exposed us to the wealth of the art that was your professional life. And that helped us to develop ourselves. I grew up to understand your vision of cinema: for you, films were not merely entertainment, somewhere they were to nudge the spectators to think of the human condition.

Whenever I think of this vision, I feel nostalgic. I remember that beginning as a reluctant actor you rose to the peak of stardom in the world of cinema. I remember your winsome smile and twinkling eyes. I remember the moments you spent with us, and thank the powers that be for the priceless legacy you have left behind for us—your family, your friends, your fans.

Let me end with the poem you so loved to recite:

> *Across the field of yesterday*
> *He sometimes comes to me—*
> *A little boy just back from play*
> *The boy I used to be...*

Bharti Jaffrey

PREFACE

Ashok Kumar. The name epitomises the very best in the craft of acting. From a young romantic to the matured hero, to an ageing character actor—Ashok Kumar has played every role to perfection.

More importantly, Ashok Kumar was instrumental in liberating Hindi commercial cinema from theatricality. He continues to do so. Earning sobriquets like evergreen, veteran, thespian.

8 February 1951. I shall remember the date forever. The place: a palatial building at Worli Seaface. When my turn came, Bimalda—the peerless director—introduced me to the inimitable hero: 'And Mr Ganguli, this is Shri Nabendu Ghosh, a renowned young progressive Bengali writer.'

'Progressive! That's a good word,' said Ashok Kumar with a kind smile. 'Welcome Nabendu Babu.'

I bowed and shyly muttered: 'Thank you but don't call me Babu.'

With a twinkle in his eyes, he said: 'Don't you worry, I shall soon throw away the unnecessary nouns and adjectives.'

Everyone laughed along with me and looking at Ashok Kumar in flesh and blood, memories took me back in time.

The year was 1936. I was then in Patna, studying for my BA exams. The ideals of Ramayan were still active in Hindu society, that is why the tragic figure of Devdas seemed acceptable to us, for few young men of the period would revolt against their parents who would not let them marry the girls they loved. Theatres and 'bioscopes'—as movies were then termed—were also prohibited for most of us. But of course we had been tasting those 'forbidden fruits' every now and then.

Then suddenly we came alive to the name of a new Hindi film that was all around us. It was being uttered by viewers, discussed in the dailies, reviewed by the magazines—the name was *Achhut Kanya*, the new film from Bombay Talkies, directed by a German director, Franz Osten and produced by one Himanshu Rai. The heroine was Devika Rani, a relation of Nobel-laureate Rabindranath Tagore and wife of Himanshu Rai, the proprietor of Bombay Talkies. The hero was a new actor named Ashok Kumar. Both the hero and heroine were charming, and the film was a super hit.

Lured by all this, we forced our way up to the booking counter of the theatre and earned our tickets. We sat in the hall. The film began at the right time and we were moved by the story that unfolded around the accursed caste system and the sin of untouchability. The heroine, Devika Rani, won our hearts at once; so did the hero, Ashok Kumar. Their actions, reactions, and dialogue deliveries were absolutely realistic and sounded very refreshing. It seemed charged with greater emotional impact than films starring other established actors and actresses of the time.

We were particularly struck by Ashok Kumar's genuine innocence as compared to the sophisticated 'innocence' of Devika Rani. Yet we would laugh and mimic Ashok Kumar's dialogues, in particular the duo's most popular song, 'Main banki chidiyan banmein ban-ban boloon re'e'e'. We lovingly caricatured his drawback, a remote effeminacy that trailed his voice.

The years rolled by, that Ashok Kumar of *Achhut Kanya* grew up, turned adult and more male—until he went beyond being a purely romantic hero and earned extra adoration as the roguish hero of *Kismet*. His acting ability acquired new dimensions and in his next film, *Najma*, he attained histrionic maturity. We on our part became his ardent admirers—nay, devotees.

More years passed and life was seized by turbulence. I lost my government job in the Bihar secretariat by writing *Daak Diye Jaai*, a seditious novel in Bengali based on the 1942 movement. The novel also placed me among the important writers of Bengal, and when I saw no hope of getting another job under the British government, I migrated to Calcutta to be a full-fledged writer. There, in 1946, unexpectedly and dramatically, I got connected with films and came in contact with the topmost director of Bengal at the time, Bimal Roy.

His *Udayer Pathe* still remains a landmark in box-office success. For the first and last time in my life I had seen something fantastic: I saw books bearing the film's title being displayed along with cigarette packets in the paan shops of Calcutta. People bought it along with their paan and cigarette! Bimal Roy had read my writings by then and had liked them. Soon he became 'Bimalda' to me.

At this point of time politics was shaping our destinies. Partition had come through but the aftermath had just about started. In Bengal, Hindus from the eastern sections were fleeing their land of birth to seek refuge in West Bengal, crowding, in particular, the streets of Calcutta. The plight worsened when Urdu was declared the lingua franca of East Pakistan—erstwhile East Bengal—and Bengali books and movies from West Bengal were banned. Those immediately affected by the move were writers and film-makers: history had brought us to a crossroad in life, for both publishing and film-making suffered a setback and came to a standstill for a while.

At that moment in time Bimalda got a call from Bombay: Ashok Kumar was inviting him to direct a film for Bombay Talkies. After giving me the news, Bimalda looked questioningly at me. 'Would you like to go to Bombay with me? Of course, it will be very difficult in the beginning and life will be uncertain...'

I did not let him complete the sentence. 'Yes, Bimalda, yes, I shall take the risk but would love to work with you.'

When Bimalda's unit started to sit on the script for Bombay Talkies it comprised of late Asit Sen, the inimitable comedian and character actor who was Bimalda's chief assistant; Hrishikesh Mukherjee, his editor cum assistant; Paul Mahendra, a distinguished actor on the payroll of New Theatres who had opted to be an assistant to Bimalda; and me, the screen-playwright cum assistant.

On 8 February 1951, we landed in Bombay with Bimalda and were later asked by Ashok Kumar to have dinner with him at his Worli Seaface residence. The man whom I had been watching on the silverscreen for the last sixteen years was before me, in flesh and blood! The man whom I once dared to mimic by singing *'Main banki chidiyan ban-mein ban-ban boloon re'e'e'...!'*

The script we wrote in Calcutta was made into a silver jubilee hit film, *Maa*, with Leela Chitnis, Bharat Bhushan, Shyama, Nazir Hussain and Paul Mahendra in the cast. No, Ashok Kumar was not in that film made for Bombay Talkies. But subsequently I wrote several scripts which featured the thespian. Among them are *Kafila*, directed by Arabind Sen; *Parineeta*, and *Bandini* directed by Bimal Roy; *Shatranj* directed by Gyan Mukherjee; *Baadbaan* and *Akashdeep* directed by Phani Mazumdar; *Aansoo Ban Gaye Phool* directed by Satyen Bose; and *Sharafat* directed by Asit Sen.

I also directed two episodes on the life of Ashok Kumar for Doordarshan's television serial, *Anmol Ratna*.

It is forty-four years since 1951, the year I got to know Ashok Kumar, and in these years I have earned his affection. During these years I read about Dadamoni, heard about him from others and learnt about him from himself. This book is the result of all that learning, written in the hope that it will afford our viewers a closer look that will reveal the great person the actor is.

My thanks to the patronage by HarperCollins. I also acknowledge the help I received at various stages from Ashok

Kumar's biography in Bengali, *Jeevan Naiya*; from *Green to Ever Green*, published by the Directorate of Film Festivals; from Firoze Rangoonwalla, in enriching this volume visually; from my son, Dipankar Ghosh; and from my dear daughter, Ratnottama Sengupta.

My thanks, above all, to Ashok Kumar himself.

Nabendu Ghosh
September 1995

CHAPTER 1

DISCOVERY OF A HERO

The gentleman was clad in a European suit. He had a sharp nose and his face was shaped like a paan—betel leaf—or, rather, a triangle. He was staring at the young man who was relishing his smoke standing in the verandah of the laboratory. The gentleman was watching the young man with a frown and a penetrating gaze, scrutinising him as if assessing him anatomically too.

The young man dragged at his cigarette for the last time and while throwing away the stub, his eyes caught sight of the man. God! That was the Managing Director! And he was staring at him with a frown! Was he critical of his smoking? He had no business to take offence for he himself was fond of smoking and was always holding a tin of State Express 555. He had no moral right to disapprove of smoking, had he?

The young man feigned he had not noticed the Managing Director. He returned to his chair inside the lab and went back to work. But an uneasiness gnawed at him with a question: Why had the gentleman fixed him with a searching gaze? What could be the blessed reason for the frown?

Suddenly his sixth sense signalled a message: the MD was still after him. Apprehensively he turned towards the door and froze. God! The Big Man was standing in the door frame, still wearing that quizzical stare. Damn it, what flaw had the respectable gentleman discerned in him?

Suddenly, wanting to put an end to the suspense, he stood up and faced the gentleman. 'S-sir, what can I do for you?' he blurted out.

The MD gravely said: 'Do as I say.'

'S-sir?'

'Walk from this wall to the opposite.'

'Walk?' The young man failed to understand, 'But why must I walk sir?'

'Because I would like to see you walk,' the gentleman said. 'Come on, walk young man.'

The young man obeyed.

'Stop now, that's enough,' the MD said approvingly. 'You suit my needs.'

'Your needs?' The young man was puzzled.

The MD smiled as he said, 'You have to act in my next film.'

'Act!' The young man was shocked.

'Yes, yes, you are going to be the hero of our next film,' the MD's smile broadened.

'Me—a hero!' The young man sounded scared, 'Oh no, sir!'

'Of course yes!' the MD was emphatic.

The young man didn't at all look pleased. 'Don't count on me, sir,' he said, 'I won't be able to do it.'

The MD's frown came back. 'Pray why not?'

The young man could not give the real reason. His father was negotiating his marriage and surely the talks would break off when the girl's family learnt that the groom-to-be was an actor. Instead, he said, 'Sir, those who act belong to the lower strata of life.'

'You know my wife acts. Do you think she belongs to that class?' the MD roared.

The young man tried to protest. He did not refer to his wife who was an exception, he tried to say, but the MD roared again, 'Don't you know that our technicians are highly educated people? Don't you know that our motto is to recruit only educated people?'

The young man felt subdued by the logic and swallowing his real feelings he meekly said, 'All right sir, try me if you like but I don't think I will suit your purpose.'

Once more the MD roared, 'Leave that to me, young man—I pick up someone only when I am confident.' With that he lit one of his 555s with a flourish.

'As you wish, sir, but I don't feel confident,' the young man made a last bid before giving up the struggle.

'I do not care about your self-assessment. It is my job to take good work out of you. Now get set—the shooting will start in four days and that's the last word on the subject.'

The MD sauntered off, a relaxed expression on his face as he puffed on his 555. The young man dashed to the recording section and reported the entire episode to his brother-in-law. 'The managing director wants me to act as a hero—' he spurted out. 'Tell me, how can I avoid the catastrophe?'

The brother-in-law, a powerfully built person, laughed out loud. 'Wonderful,' he said, 'you are a lucky chap! And thank your stars that Najmul Hussein has disappeared without notice and you have got this rare chance. Good luck!'

To put an end to the suspense: We are in 1935, on the premises of Bombay Talkies, situated in suburban Malad, in Bombay. The young man is Ashok Kumar Ganguly, the Managing Director is Himanshu Rai, founder of Bombay Talkies, and the brother-in-law is Sashadhar Mukherjee, the recordist who was to turn into the successful producer S. Mukherjee. Names that have created film history.

Of these names, Ashok Kumar of course continues to be the most popular. In 1936 Ashok Kumar Ganguly became simply Ashok Kumar, setting a trend that saw many a hero sport 'Kumar' as their surname. Kumar in Sanskrit means one who isn't married but since Ashok Kumar, it has come to mean an evergreen personality—which is perhaps what every film hero hopes to be. Thus we have had a parade of 'Kumars'—Dilip Kumar, Rajendra

Kumar, Raaj Kumar, Uttam Kumar, Manoj Kumar, Sanjeev Kumar...

In the six decades since he started acting, the name Ashok Kumar has got dearer with every appearance. And to date, he has acted in more than 300 films. The varied roles have proved not only his range as an actor but his depth too. Besides love, Ashok Kumar has earned genuine respect. The man is smiling, everywhere and all the time, jovial and affectionate. All these have made him synonymous with Dadamoni—gem of an elder brother. Ashok Kumar is the Dadamoni of the entire Indian film industry.

CHAPTER 2

HIS FAMILY TREE

Ashok Kumar is a Ganguly, which means he is a Brahmin. But he says that they are 'Amathe' Brahmins just as the Tagores of Jorasanko (Rabindranath Tagore's family) were called Pirali Brahmins. Ashok Kumar knows eight languages—Bengali, Hindi, English, Urdu, Sanskrit, Persian, German and French—but nowhere has he come across the two words 'Pirali' and 'Amathe'.

Ashok Kumar heard this from his father that they were Amathe Brahmins and descendants of the famous dacoit Raghunath, better known in West Bengal as 'Rogho of Kurulgachhi'. He emphatically says that the 'Amathes' are in reality not Brahmins at all. Rogho was the grandfather of Ashok Kumar's grandfather. He was wanted by the British police for many years and when the police came to arrest him inside a temple, they found only an elderly Brahmin and left the temple without arresting him. Since then Rogho gave up his raids and profession. And his lineage came to be accepted as Brahmins. Nothing more is known or written about him.

This dacoit Rogho is as famous a name in Bengal as Robin Hood is in England. He is remembered in literature. Rabindranath Tagore's collection of poems, *Shesh Saptak*, has one named '*Pilsujer Upar Pitaler Pradeep*' (The Brass Lamp on an Ornate Stand). He writes about a group of children seated on a mat spread out on the floor, listening wide-eyed to stories being narrated in the chiaroscuro created by the dim light of a brass lamp on an ornate stand. The narrator is old Mohan Sardar, his long hair dyed black, and he is telling the children about Rogho Dacoit.

Rogho was passing through a village, with his men carrying the loot, when he heard the wail of a mother whose daughter was dressed as a bride. As soon as she recognised him, the poor woman ran to him and, kneeling, appealed:

'I cry to you for help, O father;
save my daughter from disgrace—help, O help!'
Rogho at once appeared like a messenger of Death.
He dragged the bridegroom out of the palanquin
and struck a resounding slap
on the cheek of the groom's dad.
The man reeled on the ground...

In the courtyard once again
Sounded the auspicious conch,
And as the night trembled with joyous ululation
Rogho stood around the pandal with his men
Like the ghosts and goblins
At the wedding of Lord Shiva.

The marriage was completed. And
During the last hours of the night
The fierce dacoit said to the bride:
'Thou art my mother. If ever
You suffer any sorrow
Remember me, this Rogho.'

This Robin Hood of Bengal, celebrated by the immortal poet and living in countless such legends retold through time, is an ancestor of Ashok Kumar.

King without a Kingdom

Ashok Kumar was born in Bhagalpur, in Bihar, on 13 October 1911. His father's name is Kunjalal Ganguly and his mother's is Gouri Rani Devi, grand-daughter of Raja Shibchandra Banerjee.

As the story goes, in the middle of the last century Durgacharan, a munim (accounts clerk) in the estate of Krishna Nagar in Bengal, shifted to Bhagalpur following a quarrel with his master. He became a teacher and saw to it that his son Shibchandra got a master's degree in Law from the Calcutta University. He was bracketed first along with Bankim Chandra Chatterjee who later on turned into a literary giant and wrote the national anthem *Vande Mataram*. Both were first class firsts, and the British government offered the post of Deputy Magistrate to both of them. Bankim Chandra accepted the job but Shibchandra refused. Instead, he started to practice at the local bar council and earned Rs 40 lakh in twelve years. In terms of modern exchange rate, it would surely equal many millions.

Shibchandra would spend money freely and wholeheartedly in erecting ghats along the Ganga at Bhagalpur, besides parks, ponds, temples, schools and in many more ways to serve the people. The British government, in appreciation of his extraordinary services, proposed to confer on him the title of Raja Bahadur. But only on one condition: he would give up his practice at the bar for the rest of his life. Raja! Raja Bahadur Shibchandra Banerjee! The Britishers built him a mansion and called it 'Rajbari' (Palace). A popular saying about him started doing the rounds: *Dhol na dhaak, Angrezi baaja / Raj na paat, Shibchander Raja* (With no drum nor beat—such is the English band; with no throne nor kingdom is Shibchander a monarch).

That was to signal changes. The elated Raja Shibchandra sailed to England and there he was seized by a crazy idea: he must convert into Christianity. 'Oh, how compassionate is Christ! I must become a Christian,' he would chant day and night. He had turned raving mad.

After a few years, he returned to India but his condition did not improve. Yet he became an attraction for the European community. Raja Shibchandra—a wonderful Babu who wants to be a Christian! The Britons of Bhagalpur used to visit the Raja seated in a silver-plated carriage drawn by four magnificent horses. And the Raja, while extending regal hospitality to them, would keep saying: 'I am soon going to be a Christian. Yes, very soon.'

The Raja's insane declarations provoked the local Brahmins, they decreed that the Raja must atone for blaspheming Hinduism.

The mad Raja heard about the indictment and laughed out loud. 'Nonsense!' he said, 'Why must I atone? I am a Christian, it is only the Hindus who atone.' Further provoked, the Brahmins retaliated by pronouncing the Raja and his family as outcasts. The Raja doubled with laughter and thumbing his nose at them said, 'I care two hoots! A Christian does not care for the Hindu decree.'

One day, when the spell of insanity was at its peak, the Raja swam across the Ganga from Bhagalpur and reached Monghyr, about 40 miles away. There he sat inside a church and started to chant, 'I want to be a Christian, O please convert me and make me a Christian! Please, please.' A group of relatives in search of the Raja at last reached there and led him back to Bhagalpur.

His insanity could not be cured.

A new symptom developed thereafter. He would call his servants. 'Come here, Jagai, listen to me. Modhu, come hither and read out today's newspaper to me.' Modhu would respond by reading from the newspaper, non-stop for an hour or two, and then he would slip away on some pretext or the other. Once again the Raja would implore: 'Gour, O Gour, do you hear me, Gour? Please come here and read out the paper to me! Gour, Modhu has run away, the sly one—'

Even his own men and servants started to avoid the Raja. Gradually his health broke down.

The Britishers of Bhagalpur stopped their visits. No more would the silver-plated coaches, each driven by four horses, trot into Rajbari. The Raja would sit alone, unattended. God alone knew what thoughts crowded his mind.

Once when he would sit down to his meal, the ladies of the household would sit around him, two of them busy working the palm-leaf fans. No more: none sat by him now. Raja Shibchandra had to swallow the morsels all by himself. His eyes had dimmed and a fearless cat would pinch his share of the fish off his plate. 'Is there anyone nearby? Where has the fish disappeared?' Then, as his eyes fell on the cat he would shout: 'Jagai, the cat's off with my fish—Gour, O Gour!' But no one would listen, no one would come.

Perhaps even a mad man prays for early death. And death came at last.

He was brought to Calcutta, to a house on Hazra Road. Ashok Kumar, then only six years old, had come there with his mother. There was a crowd of relatives surrounding the Raja, he recalls.

But the Raja died without becoming a Christian.

Some seventy years since then, when a reference was made to Raja Shibchandra on June 1986, Ashok Kumar said, 'The Raja, my great-grandfather on my mother's side, had been outcasted by the Brahmins. Though we are not Brahmins, we are outcastes. My wife Shobha is a descendent of the immortal Brahmin Pundit Iswar Chandra Vidyasagar. The great soul who had fought widow remarriage was also outcasted by the Brahmins. We are jointly and completely a family of outcastes.' Ashok Kumar laughed loudly as he said this, but there was a trace of bitterness in that laughter. Abruptly he stopped and said gravely, 'This caste-system, this has spoilt everything, most of the ills of modern Indian history have their roots in this inhuman system.'

Ashok Kumar is capable of such a statement, for he inherited this attitude from his father, Kunjalal. In 1922, when Gandhiji made a passionate appeal for Hindu-Muslim unity, Kunjalal was so moved that one day he did not attend the court (he was an advocate then practising at Khandwa in Central Provinces). Instead he invited his Muslim friends, set up chairs and tables in the bazaar, and started to have khaana with them. The orthodox Hindu society saw red and and ran to the scene in the guise of friends and relatives. 'Don't do this Kunjalal!' 'What a shame Kunja Babu!' 'You are a Brahmin Brother Kunja, YOU ARE A BRAHMIN—''Don't talk nonsense,' Kunjalal retorted. 'The country has gone to dogs due to the sins of Brahmins—it is their duty to bring back sanity. For, without integration this country is doomed.'

In Search of a Sturdy Son-in-law

Ashok Kumar's mother Gouri Rani Devi was the daughter of Satish Chandra Banerjee, son of Raja Shibchandra Banerjee. Satish Chandra used to worry about Gouri Rani's health, she was very delicate in her early youth and would often fall sick. Satish Chandra used to say to his friends, 'My son-in-law must be a strong man, he must possess solid health.' When Gouri Rani came of age, Satish Chandra went to Calcutta in search of a suitable boy. One day, while passing by the Law College with his friend Ram Babu, he noticed a sturdy young man coming out of the examination hall with ink-besmeared fingers. Satish Chandra was struck with the youth's excellent physique and his confident gait. He said to his friend, 'Ram, please follow the young man and find out if he is a Brahmin and his whereabouts.'

Ram Babu followed the young man and soon overtook him. He called out, 'Listen, Tarak—' The young man turned around: 'Are you calling me, sir?'

'Yes, of course, Tarak!'

'But you are mistaken, sir,' the young man smiled, 'I am not Tarak.'

'Really?' Ram Babu bit his tongue. 'But your appearance is strangely similar to Tarak's. Anyway, what is your good name, son?'

After a while Ram Babu returned to the waiting Satish Chandra and reported, 'The young man is a Brahmin—a Ganguly, his name is Kunjalal, and he is from Khandwa. His father is...'

'Wonderful,' said Satish Chandra.

That very evening he set out on a journey. He reached Malda Town in north Bengal and from there he went to Pandua, a village of historical importance in Malda district. But Satish Chandra was disappointed. The local people shook their heads. No, there is none by the name of Kunjalal Ganguly. There is one Rangalal Ganguly, aged forty-four. There are two Kunjalals but one is a Maity and the other a Mandal.

At that moment of frustration Satish Chandra suddenly remembered that Ram Babu had said the boy was from Khandwa, not Pandua.

He went back to Calcutta and learnt that in the Central Provinces there was indeed a town called Khandwa. Very far away but it did not matter, for that Kunjalal was a very suitable boy for his daughter.

Satish Chandra reached Khandwa and staying in a hotel behaved like a trained detective and gathered information about the Gangulys. He learnt that Kunjalal takes good care of his health, he used to wrestle regularly in the past. Once the world-famed physical culturist and wrestler Sandow was ready to take him to Europe as a member of his troupe but his father's stern 'No!' had prevented that. He also found out about the parents and other family members.

Satish Chandra returned to Bhagalpur and told his family that Kunjalal is a very good boy but they are just ordinary, middle class. But Gouri Rani was destined to be Kunjalal's wife, so after many a deliberation Satish Chandra ultimately gave away his daughter to Kunjalal.

The year was 1902.

Satish Chandra Banerjee of Bhagalpur gifted a cash amount of Rs 27,000 and told Kunjalal, 'Now start your practice without any tension, my son.'

Rs 27,000 of 1902 will amount to how much in 1995?

CHAPTER 3

THE ACTOR WHO COVERED HIS FACE

The Rajbari of the Banerjees at Bhagalpur was built on a sprawling land of 20 acres that stretched from the main road to the bank of the Ganga. The area was known as Adampur Mohalla. There were some small bungalows on the land outside Rajbari. Ustads of classical music would come and stay there and music conferences would be held. Raja Shibchandra and his son Satish Chandra, usually called 'Kumar Saheb', were both patrons of art and culture. Satish Chandra had formed the Adampur Dramatic Club which was the first of its kind in the region. Writers and dramatists of all-India fame used to visit Rajbari and stay in the bungalows.

Novelist Upendranath Gangopadhyay would visit the Adampur Palace with his young nephew Sarat, who was to later turn into the immortal novelist Saratchandra Chattopadhyay. He once acted in a play titled *Bilva Mangal*, written by the legendary dramatist Girish Chandra Ghosh, in the female role of Chintamoni. Another stalwart of theatre, D.L. Roy, the unique short story-writer and novelist Banaphool (of *Bhuvan Shome* fame), the eminent writer of children's stories, Hemendralal Roy, were all associated with Rajbari in its days of glory.

Most of Ashok Kumar's early years were spent at Bhagalpur.

The holidays found him visiting his 'royal' ancestors—maternal grandfather and great grandfather—with his mother. He often met the stalwarts who visited Rajbari. He would watch a stage being erected in the courtyard, he would sit through the rehearsals of dramas that were held in a hall meant only for the Adampur Dramatic Club. Later the same plays would be enacted in the spacious courtyard of the Rajbari.

Little Ashok, when he was six or seven, used to wander about in and around the place along with his cousin Arun. This son of his mother's younger sister was junior to him by a year, which made them more of friends who would confide in each other. They would wander through the many chambers and halls, they would confer in solitary corners of the garden, they would sit and talk, dream and mimic songs.

That cousin, Arun Kumar Mukherjee, grew up in later years to be a playback singer of Bombay Talkies. And it was he who scored the music for *Parineeta* directed by Bimal Roy and also composed for *Abhimaan* directed by Joglekar. Both were produced by Ashok Kumar. When fortune smiled and *Parineeta* became a success he suddenly died, an untimely death. He was driving home, with Ashok Kumar seated by his side. They had come out of a mini projection room after watching some rushes. While talking to Dadamoni he suddenly clutched at his heart.

'Oh—oh—' he cried out in pain.

'What's that, Arun?' queried an anxious Ashok.

'Pain—in—chest—Steering,' Arun muttered, breathless in pain.

In a flash Ashok Kumar drew closer to Arun and as he took the steering Arun Kumar's head drooped. Ashok Kumar's dear cousin and childhood friend was dead. At forty-five, the sweet-tongued gentle soul had not a single enemy, and had many a tune within him that was yet to be recorded.

The child Ashok Kumar was imaginative and could tell stories to his maternal great grandfather, the Raja.

'Come on boy, tell me a new story,' the Raja would smilingly demand.

The five-year-old would gravely start: 'You see great-grandpa, yesterday I was walking through the jungle—'

The Raja's eyes narrowed. 'At what time?' he intercepted.

The boy did not lose his nerve. 'Yesterday, when you were having a nap after your lunch,' he kept up the grave tone.

'And where was the jungle?' the Raja quipped.

The boy smiled, 'On the bank of the Ganga.'

'Carry on,' said the Raja.

'As I walked through the jungle,' little Ashok went on, 'there were birds chirping and peacocks dancing. I was feeling fine when suddenly I heard a tiger roar. I stopped. The birds stopped chirping, the peacocks flew fast and in panic I turned around. And there it was standing, the tiger. It was a huge tiger, snarling at me and thrashing its tail on the ground…

'Trembling in fear I broke into a run. The tiger roared and sprang at me. I ran and ran hard. The tiger chased me. It almost reached me, it would soon fall upon me, grab me, swallow me. What shall I do? Oh, how shall I save myself? I prayed for wings and they sprang out of my two shoulders and I flew upward through the trees and escaped in the air. The tiger stopped, and roared, and roared on…'

Little Ashok looked at the Raja for a due appreciation.

But the Raja looked at him with disbelief in his eyes and asked: 'So you can grow wings out of your shoulder?'

The boy stared at him and nodded, 'Yes, I can.'

'Show me,' the Raja demanded.

Undaunted the boy said: 'You become a tiger and I will show you my wings.'

The Raja roared with laughter. 'Bravo my little one, bravo,' he conceded.

Two servants peeped in at this moment on hearing the Raja's laughter. The Raja beckoned one of them in.

'Jagai, go to Upen Ganguly's house and call that dark chap—you know—' Raja Shibchandra ordered.

'Yes, master.'

Soon a young man came there. He was dark but attractive, with handsome features and exceptionally bright, penetrating eyes.

The Raja welcomed him, 'Come here, my lad. Do you know my great grandson Ashok?'

'No sir—but now I will know him,' the dark young man smiled at little Ashok and added, 'Ashok is the name of an Emperor.'

The little boy smiled back at the compliment.

Shibchandra said to the young man, 'Look here—my great grandson is no less than you—he can also tell stories. Tell him a story Ashok.'

Before starting to narrate a story Ashok looked at the young man and asked, 'Have you ever eaten silver rice and fried silver parval?'

'I will eat them when I find them,' the young man smiled.

Many many years later, when the cinema houses displayed a 'House Full' board everytime an Ashok Kumar film was released, New Theatres of Calcutta invited the actor to join the concern. It had earned the reputation of producing quality films—and to this day the name remains nonpareil in the history of Indian cinema.

Ashok Kumar agreed to meet them to discuss the matter. When he met Birendra Nath Sarkar, the managing director, in his office there were some other directors and a dark man with silvery hair and sharp, burning eyes.

Mr Sarkar introduced the gentleman in dhoti-kurta by saying, 'Mr Ganguly, he is our pride, Shri Sarat Chandra Chatterjee, the great novelist.'

Startled, Ashok Kumar turned towards the legend and bowed low.

Sarat Chandra smilingly asked, 'Do you remember me?'

Ashok shook his head, 'No, sir—sorry.'

Sarat Chandra laughed and said, 'Try and you will remember that you used to narrate stories to me—of silver made rice and fried silver parval.'

And the scene came back to Ashok Kumar. So, he used to narrate stories to this great magician—story-writer Sarat Chandra!

Everyone had a hearty laugh when Sarat Chandra narrated the story from the past. In his turn Ashok Kumar narrated how Sarat Chandra's uncle, the writer Upen Ganguly, would regretfully say, 'This chap, my nephew Sarat, does nothing—I am worried about him.' This unleashed another round of laughter.

Ashok Kumar finally only acted in one film, *Samar*. He did not join New Theatres. It was Bombay Talkies that had groomed him and made him what he was. He would never leave Bombay Talkies.

One evening, something strange took place.

Adampur Dramatic Club was to stage a play. It was based on *Mantra Shakti*, a very popular Bengali novel written by Anurupa Devi. As the name suggests, it was about the power of Mantras, chants that bind a Hindu husband and wife in spite of temporary differences.

The auditorium was rapidly filling up. The petromax lamps had brightened up the area all around. The stage was set and upon the Drop Scene Goddess Venus was playing with her child Cupid.

Ashok Kumar, then eleven, was as usual loitering about with his inseparable cousin Arun Kumar when a member of the dramatic club called Ashok and took him to the director of the play.

They needed someone to act as a passenger seated on a bench on the railway platform and reading a newspaper. The audience, already there for an hour, was getting truly impatient.

The director was not at all pleased at the sight of a small boy to play that silent role. He needed an adult.

'He's a mere boy!' he snapped at the assistant.

'So what Dada,' the assistant argued, 'little boys also read newspapers these days.'

Some voices came hurtling from the auditorium. 'Drama-Babus, if you don't start now, send us our beds for the night—'

The auditorium resounded with guffaws and catcalls.

The director looked at Ashok. 'Look here boy, you are the great grandson of the Raja and must give a sterling performance. You have no dialogue, yet your role is important. You must convey that you are absolutely absorbed in your newspaper, okay?'

The boy merely nodded.

The final bell rang and the drop scene rolled up to reveal the railway station. There was a bench on one side and sitting on it, Ashok was reading the newspaper.

A man and a woman hurriedly passed from one end of the stage to the other.

A ticket collector walked in from the far end and made his exit by the opposite side. Off-voices floated in, calling out, 'Coolie—Coolie!'

The boy continued to read the newspaper and the audience started to get interested in him.

'Look at that boy reading a newspaper.'

'Who is he?'

Ashok looked up at the auditorium. There was Arun smiling at him, he waved his hand and giggled too.

Ashok lifted the newspaper and half covered his face.

'What's his name?'

'Arre, he is the grandson of Kumar Saheb.'

'Ashok, where would you go? Calcutta or Delhi?'

The auditorium laughed uproariously.

Ashok covered his face fully by firmly planting the newspaper in front of him.

Laughter.

'Why do you hide your face, O Ashok—'

More laughter.

The director shouted from the wings: 'Don't make fun ladies and gentlemen, s-i-l-e-n-c-e-'

Yet the laughter continued and Ashok remained seated in that state, his face covered.

He uncovered his face after fourteen years, in 1935, in a film titled *Jeevan Naiya*.

CHAPTER 4

BIOSCOPE WAS WONDERFUL

Most of those who make it in life have someone behind them. The parents are normally the first to contribute to the rise. Their characters mould their children, their qualities shape the intrinsic abilities. The rest is the sum total of one's life's deed, his or her Karma.

Ashok Kumar's father, to speak the truth, was a poor man as compared to his spouse. As a consequence, he had no time for the children, concentrating as he did on his practice at the bar and on how to make the family financially comfortable.

His mother on the other hand was like a princess. Born into a very rich family, Gouri Rani was unaware of many things, yet she managed everything wonderfully well. She was an absolute novice in the kitchen but none could detect that from her cooking. She purchased books on the art, experimented in the kitchen and rehearsed before putting the dishes on the table.

She was an exceptional lady, the unobtrusive Gouri Rani. She was one of those first Indian women who studied English as a child. A governess, Miss Annie, was brought over from England for the purpose. As a result, she was conversant with folk tales as much as she was with English classics, including Shakespeare and Chaucer. These she would read out later to her own children.

While talking about his mother Ashok Kumar relates an incident. Once while returning to Bombay by train a tiny piece of iron got into his right eye. Following an operation to remove it he went to Pune for rest. On the way, at the Victoria Terminus, he purchased some books which included an Arthur Conan Doyle novel. While reading it, the solution to the mystery dawned on him long before he reached the end. 'In a flash I remembered that I had heard the story as a boy, from my mother.'

She was also the one Ashok Kumar learnt Bengali from.

Kunjalal would not let his children go out after school. But Gouri Rani would take Ashok out to see pictures that were then shown in makeshift tents. Ashok Kumar still cherishes his first encounter with cinema. He was just about ten then. Sweet is the memory of that first experience. As sweet as first love.

This was a tent in Khandwa. A publicity party used to go through the town every day, announcing to the beat of drums: 'Come come, see the revolutionary entertainment called BIOSCOPE—you have never seen anything like this b-e-f-o-r-e...'

Tempted, Ashok told his mother who agreed to take him to see Bioscope. And one day in 1922, when Mahatma Gandhi had started his Non-Cooperation Movement, she kept her promise.

Inside the tent there were separate sections for males and females. So the mother and son went to their respective seats in the separate sections.

There was a projector at one end and a white screen at the other end. On the floor in front of the screen sat the musicians with a harmonium, a violin, a dhol and a pair of tabla.

Two men armed with syringes and a bucket of water started spraying water to moisten the screen. This was done because 'the images would look shiny when the screen is wet', Ashok was told. By the time they finished, it was 6 p.m.

A man in trousers, a coat and necktie came and stood in front of the screen, bowed ceremoniously and began like a Sutradhar, the commentator in Sanskrit dramas: 'Namaskar, brothers and sisters, ladies and gentlemen...now we will start the new and sensational discovery of this age—BIOSCOPE. Look at the screen—now will start a football match.'

And the projector released a powerful shaft of light on the screen. Images sprang to life as a thrilling match ensued to take place on the silverscreen. The musicians played in rhythm to keep pace with the match. When it ended after five minutes, the excitement in the tent found an outlet in hearty clapping.

The announcer returned to stand before the screen and began with a smile, 'Bhaiyon aur behenon, ladies and gentlemen, I am sure you enjoyed the football match. Now you will watch a horse race in the maidan.'

As he bowed and left, the projector once again came alive and a superb horse race began on the screen. Smart jockeys on glistening horses riding in a dare-devil fashion. The musicians at the foot of the screen created an illusion of the horse's hooves as they galloped across the screen. Oh what thrill, what a pleasant sensation! Bioscope surely was the eighth wonder of the world! It felt strange to watch life enacted before you, and more real than a realistic drama on the live stage. The illusion of reality was complete and compelling.

Perhaps there, in that tent in Khandwa that evening, a desire to join films had germinated in Ashok unknown even to himself.

In 1950, Ashok Kumar was in Khandwa to meet his parents. He went out one day to meet a friend, and on the way back he stopped his car when a group passed by. A man in the group was beating a drum and distributing handbills while another made announcements regarding the film.

When the group drew closer Ashok recognised the speaker. It was the same man who used to announce the different items of Bioscope. That was exactly twenty-eight years ago. Ashok Kumar was thirty-eight now, and the nameless announcer too had aged. He must have been nearly sixty, crinkled with lines that spoke of his struggle and poverty. Wearing a faded coat, a cheap trouser and a necktie, he was speaking through his loudspeaker to announce: 'Listen, listen my kind brethren, please do not miss the chance to watch one who used to walk down the streets and lanes of our very own city, one who used to stay and breathe in our dear Khandwa...see ASHOK KUMAR in his unforgettable *M-A-H-A-L*...'

And the drums rolled on...

CHAPTER 5

THE BOAT OF LIFE

Kunjalal and Gouri Rani had three sons and one daughter. Ashok was the eldest, followed by his only sister Sati. Younger to Ashok by five years, she was almost a friend to him. Next was Anoop whose pet name was Alo. Fifteen years younger to Ashok, he was a talented actor who unfortunately failed to get good roles. The youngest Kishore, the inimitable Kishore Kumar, unparalleled as a comedian, immortal as a playback singer, capricious, unpredictable and lively, was younger to Ashok by nineteen years.

Kunjalal once wanted to give all his sons names that would start with a 'K'—like his own—so they were named Kumud, Kalyan and Kishore. But Kumud and Kalyan finally became Ashok and Anoop. Only Kishore retained his original name.

Ashok Kumar's education was completely controlled and guided by his mother. But in school Ashok was—in his words—'a second-class student and sometimes had to stand up on the bench'. In spite of this he passed every year. After studying in Khandwa upto Intermediate Science he went to Jabbalpore and did his BSc from there after losing a year to typhoid.

During this period, in 1932, Ashok's sister Sati Rani was married off. The groom was Sashadhar Mukherjee who later came to be known as S. Mukherjee—one of the most successful film producers of India. Hailing from a very rich and cultured family of Allahabad, he was a student of Physics and had scored brilliant marks in his MSc examination. He had studied under Dr Meghnad Saha, the pre-eminent scientist who had high hopes for two of his students, Sashadhar Mukherjee and Gyan Mukherjee. Both of them disappointed Dr Saha, for Gyan Mukherjee also turned out to be one of the Bombay Talkies greats.

At the time of the marriage, Sashadhar was unemployed but Kunjalal had liked him immensely and so the marriage was solemnised. Just as Kunjalal was the sturdy son-in-law of Kumar Satish Chandra Banerjee, so did Sashadhar become the sturdy son-in-law of Kunjalal Ganguly.

After this marriage Ashok Kumar's name Dadamoni became very popular in the entire family circle. How so? Because Sati Rani used to address him as Dadamoni, so Sashadhar also started addressing him so, and soon everyone else took that up. Just as quickly, a splendid rapport developed between Ashok and Sashadhar.

Kunjalal used to say to his children, 'You see, life is like a boat and you are seated in that. Neither the helm nor the oars are in your hand. You cannot say for certain in which direction the boat will float—whereto this boat of life will lead you.'

His father's words proved prophetic, Ashok now says.

Kunjalal wanted his son to get a first class in BSc. Ashok fell short by 2 per cent and aggregated 58 per cent marks. Kunjalal regretfully said, 'Son, you should have studied a little more. Well, I am sure you will do better in law.'

Therefore, Ashok went to Calcutta, to study Law and stayed in the same Hardinge Hostel where his father Kunjalal had once lived with a room-mate who later became the President of India—Babu Rajendra Prasad.

Now Kunjalal started to dream that his son would become a very successful lawyer and someday would sit in the chair of the Chief Justice of India.

But the boat of life went adrift...

In Calcutta the law classes were held in the mornings and ended by 12 noon. So Ashok found ample time to see Bengali films and dramas, for which he had starved in Khandwa.

He watched the powerful actor Dani Babu, son of the legendary Girish Ghosh, the dramatist who was blessed by Sri Ramakrishna. Dani Babu's performance in the eponymous role of *Bilvamangal*, as Prabir in *Jana* and as Jogesh in *Prafulla*—all plays written by his legendary father—were ranked as classics by the Bengali audiences.

Ashok Kumar had seen another actor, the young and handsome Durgadas Banerjee who was the most popular film hero too. Ashok liked him better than Dani Babu as his actions and dialogue delivery were life-like while Dani Babu sounded artificial.

He also watched Sisir Bhaduri, the peerless actor who gave up his job as a senior professor of English for the stage. One night he was acting with Tara Sundari, a leading actress of her times. In one scene Tara Sundari embraced Sisir Bhaduri—and Ashok started to perspire, feeling uneasy about the public demonstration of the intimate action!

The stage did not attract Ashok. Bioscope still seemed better to him. During those days of 'bioscope-under-the-tent' he had seen the silent films of Eddie Polo and William Desmond which were full of acrobatics. His cousin Arun also had seen some of these American films with him and he would ask Ashok to copy some of the acts—the easier ones. At that time they would dream of becoming gallant heroes.

In Calcutta he preferred to see more of Bengali films. He was immensely impressed by two films produced by New Theatres and directed by Devaki Bose—*Puran Bhagat* and *Chandidas*. An idea sprouted in his mind: Why not go in for film direction?

By then Sashadhar had already joined Bombay Talkies as a sound engineer.

It was 1934 when Ashok became obsessed with the idea of film direction and learnt about Himanshu Rai, the founder of Bombay Talkies.

Himanshu Rai's film activities had started in London of 1922 with *Goddess*. He had acted in and co-directed the silent film *The Light of Asia* in 1925 and then *Shiraz* in 1928. Both enjoyed international acclaim and box-office success.

While making his next film, *A Throw of Dice* in London of 1928, Himanshu Rai met Devika Rani, a grand niece of Rabindranath Tagore with multiple ties to Jorasanko. She was the daughter of Col Manmatha Nath Chaudhuri, the first Indian surgeon general of the Madras Presidency, one of whose brothers was the chief justice of Calcutta High Court and another was a successful lawyer. Devika Rani had gone to England on a scholarship to study music at the Royal Academy of Music and acting at the Royal Academy of Dramatic Arts (RADA). She had also studied Architecture and specialised in textile designing, and at the young age of eighteen she had been earning her living as a textile designer at a leading studio of London.

After meeting Himanshu, Devika gave up her job and joined his production unit. The ambitious silent film, *A Throw of Dice*, was being shot by English and German technicians. Devika contributed to the sets and costumes. A year after the completion of the film, Himanshu Rai and Devika Rani got married though Himanshu was older to her by twenty years.

Then the two of them moved to Berlin to study film-making at UFA Studio, Germany's topmost film-producing concern. Devika Rani mastered the art and technique under German actor-screenwriter-director G.W. Pabst, the most influential film-maker of the Weimar Republic. She also got trained in acting under Max Reinhardt, the eminent German theatre and film director still celebrated for his innovative integration of theatre design, music and choreography in stage productions. Then, together with Himanshu Rai, she acted in a play for UFA.

Thus equipped, they made *Karma*, the first Indian talkie in English. The Indo-German-British production directed by John Hunt was shot in India but premiered in London in May 1933, two years after *Alam Ara* had released in India. Everyone who saw *Karma* raved about the heroine, Devika Rani, but financially it was not a success. When the Hindi version released a year later, it proved a big success and Himanshu Rai realised his dream of setting up a well-equipped studio back home in India.

Thus was born the Bombay Talkies. It had on its board eminent lawyers and businessmen and its staff had European technicians. The most important amongst them were German director Franz Osten, cameraman Carl Josef Wirsching and sound recordist Harley. Himanshu Rai became the Managing Director and the studio aimed, in Devika Rani's words, 'to attract the best elements in Indian society to produce the highest form of art.'

With this view they set up a training school in the studio, in which they invited educated young boys and girls from cultured families. Mumtaz Ali, Sashadhar Mukherjee, Ashok Kumar, Kishore Sahu, Snehprabha Pradhan, Nana Palsikar, Amiya Chakravarty, K.A. Abbas, Suraiya, Pradeep, Dilip Kumar, Dev Anand were all discovered by the Bombay Talkies.

Ashok was to appear for his second year Law examination in April 1934. In mid-January he started to think about film direction as a career. The more he pondered on it, the less attractive a career in law seemed to him. He wrote to his brother-in-law of his inner desire. He requested Sashadhar to introduce him to Himanshu Rai so that he could get a recommendation to study Film Direction at the UFA.

Sashadhar wrote back, 'Come over to Bombay and you shall meet Mr Rai.'

But how to go? Where could he get the fare from? Ashok did not want his parents to know his plan before it matured, so he could not write to them for extra money. Besides, it would take time, and he had to go to Bombay immediately.

Therefore Ashok utilised the examination fee to be paid to the Law College—and with the Rs 35, bought a ticket that took him to Khar in Bombay, where Sashadhar was living.

On the morning of 28 January 1934, Sashadhar received him at the VT station and said: 'Welcome, Dadamoni. Rest through the day and relax. Tomorrow you have an appointment with Mr Rai.'

Malad was about 16 km from Khar by an electric train.

This suburb of Bombay, where the Bombay Talkies was located, was a peaceful place—unlike today. The studio was a ten-minute walk from the station.

Sashadhar introduced Ashok to Himanshu Rai who sympathetically listened to the shy young man's request for an introduction to UFA.

Rai was smoking—a tin of State Express 555 was on the table before him. The smoke was sweet-scented and Himanshu, smiling sweetly, said, 'Young man, I shall speak to you from my experience: Going to Germany to learn at UFA will be sheer wastage of time. Nobody will help you to pick up easily. Instead, you can learn here, in Bombay Talkies, as an apprentice.'

Sashadhar got an opportunity to live out his ardent desire—to become a Producer. And Ashok wanted to be a Director.

Rai assured Sashadhar that he was on the right track, for the present he should continue with sound recording. But to Ashok he said, 'You start with acting.'

'Acting!' Ashok could not contain his disappointment. 'But I—'

Rai smiled patronisingly, 'You are seeking my advice, aren't you?'

'Yes, sir, of course—' Ashok fumbled.

'You see,' Rai explained, 'a director must primarily develop his sense of drama. You get alerted if you begin as an actor. Technique is only for executing drama and hence secondary.'

Ashok was intelligent to see Rai's logic though the boy who had once covered his face with a newspaper started to feel uneasy.

Rai led Ashok to the German director Franz Osten who was talking to someone in the garden, and recommended the young man for acting. Osten started to converse with Ashok.

'Mr Ganguly, do you act on stage?'

'N-no sir,' Ashok hesitantly replied.

Critically assessing Ashok, Osten asked, 'Do you sing?'

'Yes, Mr Osten,' Ashok nodded happily, 'I can sing.'

'Come with me,' Osten ordered.

He led Ashok to the steps nearby. 'Sit down,' he said, 'and sing something.'

Ashok started to wonder, what should he sing? Which song?

Suddenly he remembered a classical Bhajan which he had learnt from his mother. *'Tum ho nath Jagtaran, paar karo naiyya...* O Lord, thou art the rescuer of the world, please ferry my boat across the river of life,' he sang.

Osten heard without any comment and said, 'Let's have a camera test now.'

After the test he was given some dialogue and that was recorded too. But at the end of it all Osten shook his head. 'No, Mr Rai, no good.'

Looking at Ashok he said, 'You have a square jaw, you look too young and girlish.'

Ashok suffered the indignity as Himanshu Rai silently watched. Osten asked Ashok, 'What are you doing at present?'

'Studying Law in Calcutta,' Ashok replied.

'Then go back to Calcutta and continue studying Law,' Osten pronounced.

CHAPTER 6

THE BOAT OF LIFE MOORS

Yes, Franz Osten said, 'Go back to Calcutta and continue to study law.' Saying this, he nodded at Himanshu Rai and left the room.

Ashok and a concerned Sashadhar looked askance at Rai. A 555 was burning all right.

Rai smiled and consoled Ashok, 'Don't be depressed. Osten does not know that you want to be a director, so no damage has been done. I need more educated men for my institute. You join as a trainee technician, as a camera assistant, for a director should be familiar with every branch of film-making.'

Ashok readily agreed. 'Thank you, sir,' he said gratefully.

Kunjalal showed Ashok's letter to Gouri Rani. He felt let down by the future Chief Justice of India. What kind of career will this be! Film direction? Does a director get enough money? 'And look at the cheek of the boy! He never even consulted us!' Kunjalal fumed.

'He was afraid to do so,' Gouri Rani tried to placate her husband. 'We would have said no and that would have made him unhappy for life. Moreover, it is a new kind of profession, we don't know its prospects yet. Let us wait and watch. And then, our son-in-law is also there. He is more practical and responsible, he will take care of Ashok.'

Gouri Rani's logic seemed sound. Yes, they will wait and watch.

In Bombay Talkies Ashok had started as an assistant cameraman. For convenience's sake, he started to live in a house near the studio in Malad. His salary was fixed at Rs 150 a month.

After some months he shifted to editing, as an assistant to Savak Vacha. Some more months passed, and he became a laboratory assistant. Soon he was incharge of it and his salary rose to Rs 250 although he was still an apprentice.

Ashok still remembers the thrill, the excitement and the fear that chased him when his salary was raised. He felt the money in his pocket all the way to his house. It felt wonderful, yet there was a fear gripping his heart. Every now and then he glanced over his shoulders to check if there was any suspicious character following him. There wasn't. Yet there was no escape from the fear of losing that t-w-o h-u-n-d-r-e-d and f-i-f-t-y rupees.

The house at Malad had only three pieces of furniture—a bedstead and two chairs. He sat on a chair and trembled with fear. He decided not to open the door to anyone until he had seen the face. But what if someone breaks in? What if a thief drills his way through the wall? Where would his huge fortune be safe?

Then an idea flashed through his mind. He opened a pillowcase and hid the envelope in the bowels of the cotton wool. Only then could he go off to sleep.

Waking up the next morning, he pressed to feel the inside of his pillow. Yes, the money was there, thank God.

After the morning tea and breakfast, he ran to the Malad post office and deposited the sum into his account. When he came out he was whistling to himself the chant of *'Tum ho nath Jag-taran, Paar karo naiya...'*

Eight months later.

Bombay Talkies was preparing to launch a film, *Jeevan Naiya*, with Devika Rani and Najmul Hussein. Handsome and absolute male, Najmul Hussein was a prized hero of Bombay Talkies. He was friendly with all and to Devika Rani too. But nobody knows what happened and Najmul Hussein disappeared without notice when the first set was being erected, with only four days to go before the shooting.

Ashok had heard all this but did not feel concerned. It was not his problem but that of the Managing Director, and Himanshu Rai would have to solve it.

Working in the laboratory, Ashok felt the urge to smoke. He went out to the verandah and lit a Gold Flake, his latest luxury since he took home the salary of Rs 250. He relished the cigarette down to the last puff and as he was throwing away the stub, he saw the MD watching him with keen eyes while dragging at his 555.

Ashok wondered why. Perhaps Mr Rai did not like his smoking! He hurriedly returned to his chair in the laboratory.

Rai followed him and continued to stare. But why? Why?

Because Mr Rai had decided on his own, without the approval of the director Franz Osten, to cast Ashok as the hero—in spite of his square jaw.

The boat of life had moored.

CHAPTER 7

THE LITTLE ACTOR UNCOVERS HIS FACE

Since ancient times Nats—actors or dancers—and Natis—actresses or dancing women—were placed in a special class. At the same time they were believed to have loose morals and as such were treated as social pariahs. Yes, entertainment was enjoyed by all but entertainers belonged to a different world and were generally avoided.

In the early years of the 20th century the taboo slackened, thanks to cinema and a new surge of drama movement all over the country. Still, the Indian society of the '40s was very much dominated by the orthodox attitude. As such Kunjalal and Gouri Rani were disturbed.

That Sashadhar had taken up the job of a Sound Recordist in Bombay Talkies was happy news to them. That Ashok was working in the laboratory was not bad news either. But that Ashok had taken up a hero's role was worrying the two. An actor, especially a hero, was in constant danger of being invaded by beautiful women and seduced by heroines. So they must protect their son. He must be married immediately and at twenty-two years he was old enough to enter into wedlock.

In fact they had started negotiating with one Patol Babu (that's a pet name, the real name is forgotten) whose daughter was a sweet sixteen, very comely, and studying in the 10th class. The preliminaries had been completed, only the wedding date was to be fixed.

Kunjalal was not happy with Ashok's impulsive preference for film direction and now that he wanted to be an actor, he decided that somehow he would get his son a decent government job.

Someone heard Kunjalal and Gouri Rani talk about their son's film career. Excited, he told his friends. Within a day the whole town was talking about Ashok.

Patol Babu also came to know and that very night he visited Kunjalal. 'Sorry, Ganguly Babu,' he said, 'I shall not give away my daughter to an actor.'

Next day Gouri Rani wrote to Ashok regretting that Patol Babu had refused to accept Ashok as a son-in-law. She also warned her son and instructed him not to go too close to the female artistes.

Ashok felt bad, not about losing Patol Babu's daughter but for the frustration of his good mother. He went to Sashadhar with the letter and said, 'I shall not act.'

'But your shooting will start tomorrow,' Sashadhar gravely responded. Then he smiled and added, 'I do not count Patol Babu a great loss Dadamoni. Many other Patol Babus will come forward to offer their daughters to you.'

Sashadhar was not in the least sympathetic. 'This new form of art, this cinema, will flood the world in future,' he emphasised. 'And I think you have got a wonderful chance.'

Ashok could not decide rightaway. He was called up by Himanshu Rai who handed him a copy of the script so that he would know the story and the situations.

He will not act, but where's the harm in reading the story? So Ashok read the script. It was based on a story by Niranjan Pal, the learned son of the immortal Bipin Chandra Pal, one of the early Indian freedom fighters. The camera was to be cranked by Josef Wirsching and the music was to be scored by Saraswati Devi.

The story follows along these lines: A dancing girl, anxious to bring up her child honourably, hands her over to a social worker, Mathuradas. The girl, Lata, grows up to be a beauty who gets engaged to a cultured, educated youth named Ranjit. Before the wedding, Mathuradas takes Lata to her ailing mother and there she learns about her parentage. Chand is the villain whose evil eyes fall on Lata and he kidnaps her. But his jealous lover informs Ranjit who rescues his fiancée. Lata is cautioned not to disclose the truth about her mother to Ranjit until the wedding is over. Chand walks into the wedding reception and blackmails Lata. To buy his silence Lata parts with the precious necklace Ranjit had gifted her. Chand tries to sell it to the jeweller who had made it. He recognises the ornament and getting suspicious goes to enquire of Ranjit. Lata is forced to reveal the truth. Ranjit walks out on his bride because she failed to trust her husband. Ranjit loses his sight in an accident. Lata tends him as a nurse. Ranjit feels that the nurse resembles his wife. Then when he gets back his eyesight, he recognises her and Lata learns that Ranjit by then had learnt her true identity.

A good story, Ashok felt, yet he wanted Himanshu Rai to know that he did not wish to act. So the next day he did something to wriggle out of the role.

The studio had come to life very early since shooting was to start sharp at 9.30 a.m. Punctuality was the keyword in Bombay Talkies, not the sloppy, 'chalta hai yaar' attitude. Himanshu Rai had introduced the Western view of life, the system of taking business as business. He was a real dreamer as well as a superb planner and deft organiser. He had brought in Western technicians and a technical brilliance that was missing so far in Indian films.

Josef Wirsching's photography with proper lights, compared to the imbalanced lighting that prevailed till then, was beautifully sharp. The recording of sound was clear and the sets absolutely realistic. Sets, in those years, used to be painted. The person Rai brought in as the painter was Count Von Spratti who, in his later years, became the German Ambassador to Guatemala. His sense of perspective was perfect. Each set used to be put on wheels. The moment work on a set had been completed it would be wheeled away and the next set wheeled in. The make-up incharge was a French lady, Andre Rachebean, who was married to Savak Vacha, the editor. The sound used to be direct, and it was so horrible that you had to shout for a whisper-take. Himanshu Rai brought in Fideltronik sound system from Europe and dialogue delivery became natural, life-like.

In India, as in Hollywood, the studio system prevailed. Whoever was contracted by Bombay Talkies could not work for any other producer as long as the film was not completed. Consequently the dates of artistes were no problems. The title *Jeevan Naiya* literally meant 'The Boat of Life'. And the hero was named Ashok. What a meaningful coincidence!

Ashok reported at the right hour. But Himanshu Rai was shocked at the sight of the new hero. He had a close-cropped haircut!

Authority steeped his voice as Rai asked, 'What's that?'

Ashok feigned innocence, 'What's what, sir?'

Rai frowned. 'What's the reason for this haircut?'

Ashok dared not give the real reason. 'No—I thought—that,' he fumbled for words.

Rai stopped him and calling Andre, told her to take care of Ashok's hair with a wig and crepe.

'Go, Ashok.'

'Yes—sir—but—but I want to have a word with you, sir.'

'What is it?'

Ashok took Himanshu Rai a little aside and lowered his head as well as his voice. 'Please do not ever ask me to embrace the heroine or any girl. I won't be able to enact that.'

Himanshu Rai stared at Ashok with a faint smile and queried, 'But why this fear?'

'No sir, please,' Ashok pleaded. He could not express the uncomfortable feeling he had while witnessing the great Sisir Bhaduri embracing Tarasundari on a Calcutta stage.

'Have no fear,' Rai said, 'there is no such scene in our film.'

Ashok could not wriggle out of the role and his make-up was completed on time.

On the set Devika Rani welcomed him and wished him luck.

'Thank you, madam,' Ashok mumbled and stepped back a little at the recollection of his mother's letter.

Franz Osten briefed him gravely about the scene that would be shot. He was not happy to accept a hero he had rejected last year. The young boy had now been thrust upon him by the Managing Director and he had to obey the big man who has said, 'Whatever you may say Franz, I hold a different view. I feel he will turn into a fine hero.'

Rai walked up to Ashok when he was looking at his dialogues with a blank expression. 'You look worried,' he whispered, with a smile playing on his lips.

Ashok stood up nervously. 'Oh no, sir—no,' he also tried to smile.

Himanshu Rai was a man of experience. 'Sit down, Ashok,' he kindly said, 'and don't be nervous. The scene is very simple and so is the action. You have brought a gift for your sweetheart, a gold chain, and you have to put that around Devika's neck. Very lovingly. Right?'

'Right—sir,' Ashok gulped.

'Cheers.' Rai patted him.

'Thank you, sir,' Ashok responded.

But he started to feel nervous. He looked at Devika Rani who was smiling as she talked to the cameraman. Wife of his boss! So beautiful, so sophisticated, so sure of herself. And he was to put a gold chain around her neck! Shyness parched his throat and he felt the urge to go to the toilet. His mother's words kept ringing in his ears: 'Don't go close to female artistes.'

Devika Rani came near him and said, '*Ki Ashok, ki bhabchhish?* What are you worried about? Nervous *hosh na*, Ashok... Don't be nervous.'

In Bengali, as in Hindi, one can address people in three different ways. 'Tui' is for those who are younger, or those lower in status—somewhat similar to 'you' in English. 'Tumi' is for those who stand in between respect and affection—a term used when an affinity has been found, similar to 'thou' in English. And 'Apni' is for elders and respected persons—similar to 'thou' again in English though not as specific as in Bengali.

The verbs, likewise, have three different forms for each specific form of address. Which means Devika Rani considered Ashok to be much younger to her, like a younger brother.

She was in fact older to Ashok by three-four years.

Ashok was unnerved by her proximity.

'Rehearsal—' an assistant director called out.

Ashok noticed Sashadhar inspecting the mike position. He walked up to him and asked him to leave the sets as he was feeling shy. Sashadhar replied, 'I am your brother-in-law, so there is no reason to be nervous. Moreover I have to adjust the microphone.'

Ashok went to Himanshu Rai and appealed to him, 'Please—I can't act in Sashadhar's presence, he is my brother-in-law!'

Rai, wonderful as he was, assured Ashok. 'Relax!' he said. 'Go to your room. I am sending your lunch there, we shall start from 2 p.m. And forget about Sashadhar, he will record seated in the sound room.'

And a very special lunch was sent by Rai—a share from his own lunch pack—chicken soup, roasted chicken, pudding and sweets.

But all the compliments failed to subdue his desire to run to the toilet while rehearsing after 2 p.m. No, Sashadhar was not on the sets.

Ashok was unable to put the gold chain lovingly around Devika Rani's neck. For, he was obeying his mother's instruction.

And every time he released the chain from above Devika's head, it got stuck in her hair.

'Ashok, don't get scared,' Devika smiled assuringly. 'You bring the chain above my head in an "O" form and simply drop it. It will surely land around my neck.'

'Lights'—the camera assistant shouted.

The lights were switched on.

'Start sound,' Franz Osten commanded.

'Running'—Sashadhar's voice sounded.

'Start camera,' Franz Osten said.

'Running'—Wirsching responded.

'Ready artistes'—Franz said, and ordered, 'clap.'

The assistant director holding the clapper near Ashok's face announced the take, sounded the clap and ran out of the frame.

'Action—' commanded the director.

Ashok felt the toilet beckoning him. He disregarded the call and somehow walked up to Devika Rani. The crucial moment had come, and Ashok dropped the chain. But again, it got entangled in her hair.

The shot was running. The director did not shout 'Cut!' So Ashok took a chance, pulled at the chain and it snapped into two. Simultaneously Devika Rani's hair came down in disarray.

'Cut-cut!' Franz Osten shouted. Then, without any comment, he beat his forehead.

Rai smiled as usual and said, 'My dear Ashok, how can you act if you don't ever touch a girl?'

Devika Rani giggled.

Ashok reddened like a beetroot.

Rai and Osten talked aside and decided to waive off that scene for the present and take up another.

The new scene was explained to Ashok. It was an encounter with the villain. That role was being acted by an artiste named Massey. He and Devika were to converse by the window of a room on the first floor of a building when Ashok would spring in and pull apart Massey just about to molest her.

Franz started to describe the action to Ashok.

'Mr Kumar'—he started.

Rai stood up, 'Franz, thank you.'

'Why, Mr Rai?' Osten wondered.

Rai smiled as he said, 'You have helped me give a name to the new hero Ashok Kumar Ganguly.'

'Pray what is it?' Osten asked.

'Tear apart "Ganguly" from his full name—make him a casteless hero, loved by all castes and classes,' Rai said. 'He shall be simply Ashok Kumar.'

Osten gravely said, 'I don't mind.'

Devika Rani clapped and said, 'Hail, Ashok Kumar.'

Everyone on the set clapped.

But Ashok looked worried and trapped.

'Silence everybody'—Osten resumed his instructions.

'As I was going to tell you Mr Ashok Kumar, please note carefully that from the moment you hear the clap-sound you will count ten. Massey and Mrs Rai will converse and just when you finish counting you shall jump in through the window and separate them. Shall I repeat?' Osten sounded harsh.

Ashok shook his head, 'No, Mr Osten, no.'

He thought he could tackle this part, so he disregarded the urge to go to the toilet.

'I'm ready, sir,' he said.

'I would risk a take without any rehearsal and with lights,' Osten said. He turned towards Ashok and said, 'Go and take your position behind the window.'

'Right sir,' Ashok obeyed.

'Ready everybody?' Osten said, 'Lights.'

The needed lights were switched on.

'Start sound,' Osten ordered.

'Running,' sounded Sashadhar.

'Start camera.'

'Running.' Brrrrrrrr— the camera sprang to life.

'Clap.'

Ashok shot up into the window frame and sprang upon Massey and Devika Rani. Both of them fell flat on the floor. The hero stood erect while the others groaned.

'Cut—Cut—' Osten yelled.

Everything stopped. Osten angrily faced Ashok and barked at him, 'Mr Kumar, I asked you to count ten. How could you forget that?'

Ashok guiltily said, 'I am sorry, Mr Osten.'

Devika Rani stood up before Rai could reach to her help. She started to laugh but Massey began to groan as he tried to stand up. 'I can't stand up,' he complained.

'Call our doctor—' Rai ordered 'immediately.'

The doctor came and examined Massey. His right leg had a fracture.

Osten shouted, 'Pack up.'

Rai looked at Ashok gravely and whispered, 'So you broke the villain's leg!' He broke into his usual, kind smile and walked away.

Ashok ran to the toilet.

Kunjalal was not idle about Ashok. Gouri Rani was there to goad him on to sound out his influential friends and get a proper job for their son.

Ravi Shankar Shukla—father of the seasoned politician Vidya Charan Shukla—was the chief minister of the Central Provinces and Kunjalal had known him over the years. He met Mr Shukla with a plea to rescue his son from films.

Ravi Shankar said, 'I can get him a Postal Inspector's job. In future he can rise to be the Post Master General.'

The offer did not seem very attractive to one who hoped to see his son as the Chief Justice of India. He said, lowering his head, 'Any other job, Shuklaji?'

Ravi Shankar thought for a while and said, 'Then tell him to apply for the post of an Income Tax Inspector. He can rise to be an Income Tax Commissioner. He will get a start of Rs 340.'

Kunjalal smiled, 'This sounds better Shuklaji.'

He wrote at once to his son, 'Here is a job that is respectable and paying. You shall start at a salary that is more than what you are earning as an actor.'

A month passed by.

Jeevan Naiya was making brisk progress. Ashok in the meantime had gathered confidence and was improving daily. Franz Osten looked neutral but Himanshu Rai was hopeful these days. Special lunch would come for Ashok from the MD and his wife.

Following the German system, the earlier day's shooting was seen everyday, before work. Ashok felt that his acting was amateurish.

One day Rai requested him to make greater efforts.

Ashok reacted vehemently, 'Mr Rai, I shall try my best to act better but I shall not do "theatre". I shall never give postures and poses.'

Rai smiled. 'You are correct,' he said, 'but do not underrate drama Ashok. If you do not dramatise a little, then your normal acting will look underplayed on the screen.'

Ashok took time to appreciate Rai's views. Meanwhile, he received the letter from Kunjalal.

He took the letter to Himanshu Rai.

'Good prospect,' Rai said, 'but you have signed a contract with our concern. So let the shooting be completed and we shall release you. You have to wait for only about a month, and I'm sure you will not get that job rightaway.'

Mr Rai was very reasonable.

Ashok wrote back to his father accordingly.

A month later, *Jeevan Naiya* was complete.

Whither now, O Boat of Life?

CHAPTER 8

EYES HARBOUR THE HEART

Jeevan Naiya was to be released in two days. Ashok Kumar went to Himanshu Rai and said, 'I obeyed you sir, *Jeevan Naiya* is complete. I now seek your permission to leave.'

Rai silently puffed at his 555. He stared at Ashok for a few seconds before he smiled. 'Of course you can go, for you have fulfilled your contract. But if you like you can sign another contract for a new film.'

'Thank you, sir,' Ashok replied, 'but I feel I am not fit to be a hero. I've watched myself in *Jeevan Naiya*—I'm no good. Mr Osten is not happy either.'

Rai raised his pitch as he said, 'Leave aside what the director thinks. He did not select you, I did. And I believe that you will rise to eminence. You see Ashok, everyone has to go up the stairs, step by step, to reach perfection.

Ashok's spirit was enlivened by the words. Yet he could not overcome the dilemma between his father and films.

He said, 'Give me time to think, sir.'

Rai said, 'But you must think quickly, for there are only three days to go before we start shooting the next film. The entire film is to be completed within a month. So come back in two hours' time and give me your decision.'

'To be or not to be…' Ashok thought to himself as he returned to his Malad residence. To be in films or out of them? To please his father or displease him?

He assessed the experiences of the last year and half and felt confident of his acting ability. Now the question of personal predilection stared him in the face. Inhibition and indecision had run roughshod over his confused mind for quite a while. Slowly he was discovering the thrill and joy of working in films and the very thought of wrenching himself away to something else was disagreeable to him.

That assessment led him to sign the new contract, for *Achhut Kanya*. The story was by Himanshu Rai, the cameraman was once again Wirsching, the director Franz Osten and the heroine Devika Rani. He read the script, revolving around a young woman who sacrifices herself to save others. The love of Kasturi, the daughter of a low-caste railway employee Dukhiya, and Pratap, the son of the Brahmin Mohanlal, the village grocer, is doomed from the very beginning. The orthodox villagers frown even upon intercaste dining. When Mohanlal takes the ailing Dukhiya to his home, antagonism flares into riots and Mohanlal gets injured. To bring medical aid to his friend, a fever-racked Dukhiya stops a mail train for which he is dismissed. Pratap is married to Meera and Kasturi to Manu, each into their caste. Pratap constantly thinks about Kasturi but she turns into a dutiful wife reconciled to her fate. Pratap's wife and Manu's first wife connive against Kasturi whose husband Manu is incited to kill Pratap. As the Brahmin and the untouchable youth fight on the railway tracks, Kasturi—trying to stop an onrushing train—dies but succeeds in saving two lives, her husband and the man she loves.

Ashok did not attend the premier of *Jeevan Naiya* for he had seen the film in the laboratory and considered his acting as poor.

Himanshu Rai heard about his complex. He gifted Ashok a new suit and said, 'Wear this to see the film tonight. You must face the situation. And you must not underrate yourself. Sit with the audience and you will feel better.'

Clad in the new suit Ashok went to the theatre and sat in a

box. When the show ended a gentleman came out of the adjoining box and said, 'The Maharaja is calling you. Will you please come with me?'

Maharaja?! Ashok felt curious and followed the man into the next box where a fat gentleman was sitting with his wife. He smiled as he said, 'You have done very well—we felt very happy watching you.'

'But who is this gentleman?'—Ashok wondered to himself. And, as if responding to this thought which he had read through telepathy, the man who had acted as the messenger said, 'Perhaps you don't recognise him? He is the famous Maharaja of Gwalior—Scindia.'

This acquaintance was to develop into a friendship with the Scindias later on.

Rai's words were true. Due to the audience reaction, *Jeevan Naiya* looked better to Ashok but he was far from convinced about himself. His performance was too 'underplayed'. Lifeless.

Achhut Kanya's shooting started the very next day and was completed in thirty-one days. But it did nothing to instill confidence in Ashok, he was still nervous.

Once he asked Franz Osten, 'What do you think Mr Osten, am I doing right?'

Osten evasively replied, 'Your acting will not matter. Do as you can best, it's the story that will pull it through.'

'That's right,' Rai seconded him.

Ashok was not satisfied with their replies. Well into his second film, he still felt uncomfortable with his two hands. What should he do with them while talking? While standing? While doing an emotional scene?

There was a scene where the dejected heroine says their marriage was impossible as she was an untouchable. At this Ashok clasps both his hands and wails out, 'O God, why did you not make me an untouchable?'

When the shot was over Franz Osten said, 'Mr Kumar, your two hands clasped each other so hard that it seemed they would break into pieces.'

There were many such uncomfortable situations in *Achhut Kanya*. But as soon as the film was released in 1936, it became a hit. The whole of India started to croon, '*Main banki chidiyan ban ke ban ban bolun re-e-e.*' They also started to chant a name: 'Ashok Kumar, Ashok Kumar, Ashok Kumar.'

The film was hailed for its wonderful social message. It was a milestone for Ashok, too.

Achhut Kanya attracted all sections of the populace and, finally, even Pandit Jawaharlal Nehru. He was intimate with Himanshu Rai and Devika Rani and hearing praises about the film he asked to see it when he came down to Bombay.

Arrangements were made for a special screening. Panditji, Sarojini Naidu and Indira came to the theatre accompanied by a big group of men and women. Rai, Devika Rani and Ashok sat along with the honoured three while the other guests sat in the rows behind them. The show began. Panditji and Indira watched with interest but Ashok and Himanshu Rai found that Sarojini Naidu had fallen asleep. When the film reached the situation where the hero Pratap sang '*Khet ki muli, baag ki aam*', Sarojini woke up and she said, 'Who's that boy, he's singing so well!' Ashok was sitting next to her, he said, 'That's me up there on the screen.' 'Bravo,' she said, 'Congratulations.'

Thereafter, Panditji and Indira visited Bombay Talkies many times and whenever he saw Ashok he would shout, 'Hello hero, *kaise ho*, how are you?'

Yes, no matter how imperfect, Ashok Kumar attained stardom with *Achhut Kanya*. But most of the praises for the film was showered upon his leading lady, Devika Rani, who had given a truly magnificent performance. As regards Ashok Kumar, the papers praised his pleasant personality, his infectious smile, but dubbed him a 'chocolate-hero'. And whenever people met him, they would praise him and say, '*Achha hai, achha hai, magar aur zyada dil kholkar kaam karo* (Well done, well done, but work with greater zest).'

'*Dil kholkar?* What does that mean?'

Ashok felt that whatever these people were saying corroborated what he felt about himself. Something was wrong somewhere. Sashadhar also said one day, 'Dadamoni, you have to take care of your acting. Something is missing. If you want to stay in this you must improve yourself, you must do better. If you cannot, you better leave this profession.'

In Khandwa, Kunjalal and Gouri Rani were in suspense. They were tense since Ashok had turned a hero. They had fears about the city and thought it would corrupt their son. But after *Achhut Kanya* they noticed that their son had been catapulted to the limelight. He was being widely discussed, his photographs were in the magazines and dailies, and people all around them were singing '*Main ban ki chidiyan ban ke ban ban bolun re-e-e...*' All this made them very happy and proud.

Gouri Rani could heave a sigh of relief because Ashok had, as promised, kept a little distance during the love scenes between the heroines and himself.

Himanshu Rai said, 'Don't be depressed. I must say that you are improving and will do better still. But you must start to know about things like characterisation, voice control, action, gestures and postures. To begin with, start seeing foreign films. Watch their heroes, and I'm certain you will improve. Start off today. Go and see Ronald Colman in *A Tale of Two Cities*—I'll send someone to get you the tickets.'

Rai took pains to get Ashok the tickets for *A Tale of Two Cities*. Ashok saw the film and was terribly impressed by Ronald Colman.

He discussed his acting with Himanshu Rai who pointed out certain traits of Ronald Colman which Ashok had overlooked. Rai asked Ashok to see the movie once more.

One day Devika Rani said to Ashok, 'Don't shake your head too much while acting Ashok, because it disturbs.' Ashok took note of all such observations and remembered all that was said. He now decided that if he was into film-acting, he must make a good job of it.

One day he went on a tour of Bombay's bookshops and picked up some American and European books on acting styles and technique. One of the books was titled *Rehearsal*. After going through them he found they were all about stage-acting, there was nothing about acting for the screen. Even so, he learnt how to throw his voice and control it for better effect. He noted the instruction that one should practise the gestures and postures in front of a mirror, to correct them and make them more effective.

Thereafter he started going down to the beach close to Bombay Talkies with the dialogues of the film. To improve his delivery he would speak the lines repeatedly when no one was watching. Back home, he would speak them before a mirror and decide upon the actions and reactions bearing in mind how he looked at every step.

He also made it a point to see foreign films starring the ruling deities of the time like Ronald Colman, Spencer Tracy, Leslie Howard and Charles Laughton. He would study their actions and expressions and then compare himself with them. As a result his sense of timing and naturalness showed remarkable progress.

Sashadhar used to help Ashok when he watched his own films. He himself was not an actor, but he was an excellent coach—he knew precisely what was right and what wasn't. He would tell Ashok, 'Look at your scene and your dialogue from your point of view, personalise it.'

Gyan Mukherjee, the director of *Kismet* and *Sangram*, was another intelligent person who helped Ashok with frank, constructive criticism.

Recollecting those days, Ashok compliments his unique brother-in-law, Sashadhar Mukherjee, in these words: 'The one who really trained me was Sashadhar Mukherjee. He was a superb person and, to tell the truth, if there was any intelligent man in films, it's him. If there is any award higher than the Dadasaheb Phalke award, he should get it.'

In 1936, Ashok starred in three films: *Jeevan Naiya*, *Achhut Kanya* and *Janma Bhoomi*. All three featured Devika Rani against him. The next year he starred in *Izzat* with Devika Rani, *Prem Kahani*—shot in only eighteen days—with Maya Devi and Madhurika, and lastly in *Savitri* with—once again—Devika Rani. In 1938 only two films were made, *Nirmala* and *Vachan*: both starred Ashok Kumar and Devika Rani.

All these films were enjoyable but none was outstanding. Nevertheless, the popularity of Bombay Talkies as well as Ashok Kumar soared. Even the press had started to take note of his performance though it guarded itself against going overboard with superlatives. And the actor himself felt that in spite of improvement and progress his acting still lacked something vital.

A change crept in with *Kangan* in 1939. It was based on a short story, *Rajanigandha*, written by the Akademi award-winning Bengali writer Gajendra Kumar Mitra. The film's rights was purchased for Rs 250 only!

Kangan was the last of Franz Osten's directions and Ashok was paired with a new actress, Leela Chitnis.

On the first day of shooting Ashok Kumar met Leela Chitnis for the first time. 'We are to work together,' he greeted her. 'I hope you enjoy working with me,' he added with a laugh.

While shooting, Ashok was impressed by Leela's performance. Watching her closely, he realised that she 'spoke' through her eyes. Dialogues were often not essential because her eyes would light up when she had to convey joy or they would go melancholic to express sorrow. This he learnt from Leela Chitnis, this art of how to speak with his eyes.

In her autobiography, *Chanderi Duniyet*, Leela Chitnis has recorded her feelings about Ashok Kumar of the *Kangan* period. 'He had a very attractive face,' she writes, 'beautiful eyes, a nice nose, six feet tall and a habit of talking while laughing. He projected a peculiar childlike straightforwardness—very impressive as far as the listener was concerned. However, he seemed to have a weak build, and as an actor his personality seemed unimpressive. And there was no liveliness in his eyes.'

'I remember those early days well,' she further writes. 'We then had ambivalent feelings towards each other. I used to say to myself, "He should not surpass me." And he thought likewise about me. It was a secret competition between us.'

This secret competition paid its dividend. *Kangan* became a hit. Ashok Kumar and Leela Chitnis became extremely popular as screen lovers.

All of a sudden, changes started to overwhelm the world. The Second World War affected Bombay Talkies. Franz Osten and other German technicians were deported from India.

Since 1939 Himanshu Rai was relying more on the versatile Sashadhar Mukherjee and shifting his responsibilities to him. On his part, Sashadhar had been tackling everything very efficiently. But in 1940, when everything seemed fine, catastrophe struck. Himanshu Rai had launched a new film, *Narayani*, when he suddenly had a nervous breakdown and died.

The creator of Bombay Talkies was gone and Devika Rani took over the leadership. *Narayani*'s shooting stopped. A new film, *Azad*, was launched with the same cast, Ashok Kumar and Leela Chitnis, under the direction of N.R. Acharya. This was followed by *Bandhan*, produced by S. Mukherjee and directed again by N.R. Acharya, and once again starring Ashok Kumar and Leela Chitnis. This film was another silver-jubilee hit.

In 1941 came *Anjaan* with Devika Rani and Ashok Kumar in the leads. This launched a new director whom Devika Rani had recruited—Amiya Chakravarty. The film did not do well at the box office and was the last to pair Ashok Kumar and Devika Rani.

Then came *Jhoola*, teaming Ashok Kumar with Leela Chitnis under the direction of Gyan Mukherjee. Once again a hit, another silver jubilee. This film, along with *Kangan* and *Bandhan*, turned Ashok Kumar into a matinee idol. The racy plots, the brooding camerawork and haunting music besides the performances fired the popularity of this trilogy. These, it must be added, were the precursors of the formula film as it exists till the present times.

Newspapers and magazines, that had remained appreciative of Ashok Kumar, sang his praises when *Naya Sansar* was released. It had cast Ashok with a new heroine, Renuka Devi. Once again the director was N.R. Acharya and the powerful story about a courageous and crusading newspaper reporter was by Khwaja Ahmed Abbas. Now, in the flush of success and reading the rave reviews, the generally diffident Ashok Kumar felt convinced about his maturity as an actor. A far cry from the fumbling newcomer of six years ago.

At one time people used to tell Ashok Kumar: '*Dil kholkar kaam karo.*' He had done so. At last he had opened up his heart through his eyes.

CHAPTER 9

KISMET

Ashok Kumar, by now hoisted to starry heights, was still the laboratory incharge. He was part of the creative team of Bombay Talkies, and adept at every aspect of film-making.

The creative team searched for another story that would work at the box-office. For, every film-maker knows, only that story is good which sets your heart aflutter.

Sashadhar, Ashok and Gyan Mukherjee had got hold of a marvellous book on Hollywood script-writing by Francis Marion. The book had a scene-by-scene break-up of twenty such classics, from the early black-and-white version of *The Champ* (1931) to *Ben Hur* (1925). The notes underlined the need for logic, for cause and effect. Marion stressed that in a good screenplay every scene must be gripping. He said that a film's plot should be such that it could be encapsulated in a single line.

Marion's book guided the three into framing a theme: 'A bad man gets involved with a good girl and reforms.' They then set about developing it into a story. It winds around Shekhar, a charming and chivalrous crook who is let off from the jail for the third time. On one of his nocturnal rounds, eluding the long arm of law he slips, as fate would have it, into the house of Rani, a stage actress. Not so long ago she was a successful performer. Today she is a cripple, her father has abandoned the house and she is constantly hounded by a creditor, Indrajit Babu.

Sympathy flowers into love. Shekhar takes charge of Rani's life, pays off the interest on her loan and gifts her a necklace as a token of his love.

But the happiness is soon shattered. Shekhar is arrested for the theft of the necklace. Rani is shocked. The magic of love changes Shekhar. He goes out to steal for one last time, to collect money for Rani's treatment. He burgles into Indrajit Babu's house and leaves the money for her without revealing his identity.

Shekhar is arrested but now he is assured of Rani's love. This time he comes out a new man.

The three obeyed all the instructions of Francis Marion and after a great deal of brainstorming came up with a script. The film was *Kismet*. The year, 1943.

A new heroine, Mumtaz Shanti, was cast opposite Ashok Kumar and Gyan Mukherjee was to be the director.

The shooting started. The moviola projected interesting scenes and performances. The direction looked slick. The film was completed as per the schedule.

But something was brewing in the meantime.

After the death of Himanshu Rai, Devika Rani was the leader but virtually everything was being planned, conducted and executed by Ashok and Sashadhar. Then Devika Rani started patronising Amiya Chakravarty and declared that she would decide everything. Ashok, Sashadhar and others toed the line but they also decided to leave at an opportune moment.

Sashadhar Mukherjee and Amiya Chakravarty were unable to see eye to eye. One day, while the final editing of *Kismet* was on, matters reached a flashpoint.

Ashok was supervising the editing in the laboratory when Chakravarty, now elevated to a senior rank by Devika Rani, walked in and asked to see the rushes. Then he asked Ashok to leave.

It was a calculated humiliation.

Ashok returned to his room in the lab and punched the wooden partition. His fist was smeared with blood and his eyes smarted with tears. 'Yes, I will leave,' he muttered under his breath, 'but only to return some day. Yes, I shall.'

He went to bid goodbye to Devika Rani. But he was stopped by her security guard who politely said, 'Memsahib has ordered that she should not be disturbed, by any one.'

This incident was preceded by another. Sashadhar, infuriated by many a situation and insinuation, had said to Devika Rani, 'Either Chakravarty stays or I do—you must decide today Mrs Rai.'

Devika Rani had looked up coolly. Amiya Chakravarty was her protege, so she said, 'Yes, I decide now that Mr Chakravarty will stay.' And Sashadhar had left the premises of Bombay Talkies, never to return.

Ashok Kumar also left Bombay Talkies, along with Rai Bahadur Chunilal, the general manager; Dattaram Pie, the editor; and Gyan Mukherjee, the director of *Kismet*.

In other words, the creative team of *Kismet* left and some days later, when the film was released, it became an amazing success, setting a record that would be referred to for decades to come. It ran for three years continuously in Calcutta's Roxy theatre situated in the Dharmatala area. It can be dubbed the *Sholay* of pre-Independence years.

Ashok had earned plaudits for *Naya Sansar* but *Kismet* fetched another kind of appreciation. They said his performance was so good that it might inspire the youth of the country to turn into thieves and pickpockets. They brought into question the morals of Rai Bahadur Chunilal who was a member of the Bombay Censor Board and also associated with the production. All in all, the film became a trendsetter. 'Rob the rich and help the poor'—the theme came into vogue with *Kismet* and continues to be in vogue.

With *Kismet* Ashok Kumar's career swung to greater heights. One could say, his kismet became mightier.

Dictates of Destiny

That very year, 1943, in Goregaon which is close to Malad, Sashadhar Mukherjee started a new film production concern: Filmistan. Rai Bahadur Chunilal, Gyan Mukherjee and Ashok Kumar became partners.

Their first venture was *Chal Chal Re Naujawan*. The title proved their attachment to Bombay Talkies for it was a line from a song in *Bandhan*.

When Ashok left Bombay Talkies he was drawing a salary of Rs 1000. In Filmistan he started at Rs 2000. He began freelancing with *Angoothi* which had Chandraprabha opposite him and was directed by B. Mitra. His remuneration then was Rs 20,000.

Kundanlal Saigal, the famous singing hero of New Theatres Pvt Ltd, increased his rate. So did Ashok Kumar, and producers bowed to his demand in deference to the growing success of *Kismet*. Some paid him Rs 75,000 and Mehboob Khan signed him for *Najma* at one lakh rupees. It was a mindboggling amount at the time, and that's how black money entered the film industry and the studio system died out. All this happened in 1943.

Under Gyan Mukherjee's direction, *Chal Chal Re Naujawan* continued to be made at an unhurried pace. But Ashok was contract-bound to give priority to Filmistan, all the more since he was a partner. Whenever he worked in Filmistan, he had to work during the day. That is why he worked for Mehboob's *Najma* mostly by night.

Najma was the first Muslim social. Earlier Muslim films were all of the *Thief of Baghdad* and *Alibaba Chalis Chor* variety. When *Najma* was released, Ashok Kumar's performance reached the pinnacle of success. *Najma* was a box-office hit and the demand for Ashok Kumar increased even more. It spelt more work for him.

Chal Chal Re Naujawan also released in 1943. The film had no powerful narrative base and did not have a successful run but it did establish the Filmistan banner. At the time when the normal selling price for all-India distribution was Rs 4 lakh, *Chal Chal Re Naujawan* fetched Rs 18 lakh.

Those were the days of untiring work, round the clock, day or night. Mehboob at once signed him for *Humayun* in 1945, Devaki Bose called him for *Chandrasekhar* based on a Bankimchandra classic. Kanan Devi was cast opposite him and Devaki Bose offered him Rs 2.5 lakh. Ashok had thirty films in a row.

Ashok Kumar had gone into films with the ambition of becoming a director. He fulfilled that ambition now. He directed *Eight Days* in 1946, for Filmistan. It was the story of a young armyman who refuses to get entangled in an arranged marriage. But when the film was complete Ashok changed his mind and gave the credit to Dattaram Pie, the editor.

No print of *Eight Days* is available any longer. The negative was destroyed in a fire.

During that period Ashok was also involved in the production of *The Three Headed Cobra*. All the technicians of the film in English were foreigners, working under the Hungarian director Akos Rathaoni. After its completion the technicians were paid off their salaries but they insisted on overtime dues which totalled to a hefty Rs 30 lakh. It was too big an amount to be paid off forthwith. The technicians brought an injunction staying the release of the film until they were paid. As a result *The Cobra* was never released.

Ashok acted in one more film for Filmistan. *Shikari* was directed by Savak Vacha, a colleague and editor from Bombay Talkies. The story was a riveting comedy and for its music, Sachin Dev Burman was brought down from Calcutta.

That same year, after a year's acquaintance, Devika Rani married the renowned Russian painter Svetoslav Roerich, left Bombay and bade farewell to films. Bombay Talkies was in doldrums and the news stirred up sentiments in Ashok Kumar. He approached Savak Vacha, his erstwhile guru in editing, now a partner-colleague in Filmistan, and said, 'Let's buy up the major shares of Bombay Talkies, our filmy alma mater. I have done enough acting, now I want to be a producer.'

Vacha jumped up with excitement, 'Yes Ashok, let's do it.' And they did buy up the major shares of Bombay Talkies from Devika Rani and left Filmistan.

When Ashok re-entered the premises after a lapse of five years, the company was being looked after by an employee, a lady. Ashok met her to take charge and found the plaster-cast bust of Himanshu Rai rolling on the floor, at one corner of the studio, amidst a heap of waste papers and throwaways.

A shocked Ashok picked up the bust, dusted it with his handkerchief and asked the lady, 'Would you sell this to me?'

'But why do you want to buy it?' the lady wondered aloud. 'For decoration purpose? Is it someone important?'

'Yes, madam,' Ashok replied, 'someone very important to us and to the history of Indian cinema. Himanshu Rai, the founder of Bombay Talkies. This bust needs special care.'

The lady lowered her head. 'Please take it away, please—' she muttered.

Himanshu Rai returned to his discovery, Ashok Kumar.

Ashok carried the bust to the laboratory—the room he had left in 1943. His eyes glistened as memories filled him. And a sense of joy, profound joy.

Several years later Ashok said about that day: 'When I sat in that room once again, the happiness I felt was greater than what I felt at receiving the Padmashri or the Phalke award.'

CHAPTER 10

PLAYING GOD

When Ashok Kumar and Savak Vacha took over the leadership of Bombay Talkies they shouldered the burden of Rs 28 lakh to be paid to the debtors. It was a public limited company. During the board meetings various malpractices and defalcations came to light. One of the directors had an umbrella shop and he had sold 1200 umbrellas to Bombay Talkies! Another had a sari shop and had sold several hundred saris to the company!

Ashok said to Vacha, 'We are trapped but we must steer through it carefully, we have to make films with low budgets.'

'Right, Dadamoni,' Vacha nodded gravely.

'Dadamoni'—another name for Ashok Kumar—started to circulate in the industry since then. Before that only Sashadhar Mukherjee, his wife Sati Rani and Ashok's younger brothers, Anoop and Kishore used to call him by that name.

There was a reason why Vacha started to call him Dadamoni. Earlier, when Ashok was Vacha's assistant in editing he used to call him 'Ashok'. But when Ashok turned the boss of Bombay Talkies, Vacha hesitated to address him by his name. And 'Mr Ganguly' would rob them of their intimacy. One day during this dilemma Sati Rani stopped by to visit Ashok. Vacha heard her address him as 'Dadamoni' and liked the word very much. His problem too was solved. 'Dadamoni' denoted brotherhood. It denoted both nearness and dearness, respect and love. As he started to address him as 'Dadamoni' the word was taken up by the whole industry—nay, the whole country. It resounded in the paan-shops as much as in the palaces.

They sat down to work in earnest.

Bombay Talkies had once employed a director named Nazir Ajmeri. But he never made any film: he had opted for Pakistan and shifted there after the Partition. He had once narrated a story which still lingered in Ashok's memory. So he called Ajmeri from Pakistan and out of his story started making *Majboor*, the first production under the stewardship of Ashok Kumar. The hero was an actor named Shyam and the heroine was Munawar Sultan.

This was happening in 1948, when India was convulsed with communal riots. The talents Ashok had selected for the new phase in Bombay Talkies were the acclaimed Urdu writer Sadat Hasan Manto, Kamal Amrohi, Shahid Latif, his wife Ismat Chughtai, Hasrat Lucknowi, Nazim Panipati, music director Ghulam Haider, and of course Nazir Ajmeri. All Muslims. This antagonised the Hindu workers, then traumatised by the riots and the post-Partition sense of loss.

Sadat Hasan Manto writes about the times and about Ashok Kumar in his *Meena Bazaar*. He claims to have cautioned Ashok about the feelings of the Hindu workers. Hearing him Ashok had simply laughed, refusing to pay any attention to his words.

There were threats from outside that Bombay Talkies would be burnt down. Ashok said to Manto, 'This is all madness. I am sure that everything will settle down gradually.'

Instead, the situation worsened.

One day Manto came to Ashok's house and they talked late into the night. So Ashok went to drop Manto to his house, and trying to take a shortcut he drove through a Muslim locality.

A marriage procession was coming up at that moment. Manto panicked at the thought that they might hurt Ashok since he was a Hindu. He started to pray.

The car had to stop to make way for the procession, and people recognised Ashok. They started chanting his name—'Ashok Kumar! Ashok Kumar!'

Manto was gearing up to fight for Ashok in case the crowd misbehaved, when two youths came forward and said, 'Ashokbhai, this road is blocked, please go out by the lane on the left.'

'Shukriya Bhailog!' Ashok responded and followed the direction. When they were out of the neighbourhood, Ashok laughed. 'Manto,' he said, 'people do not question artistes. They are neither Hindus nor Muslims.'

Ashok had inherited his father's faith about Hindu-Muslim integration. The riots subsided gradually as he had maintained, and when *Majboor* was released it celebrated a silver jubilee.

At the next board meeting they found out that 25 out of the 28 lakh rupees liability had been paid off. Everyone felt relieved that only Rs 3 lakh remained to be cleared.

Shahid Latif, Ismat Chughtai and Sadat Hasan Manto sat down with Ashok to create a story for the next film which was to be directed by Shahid. They all requested Ashok to play the hero opposite Kamini Kaushal. But he said nothing, only smiled. He had no desire to act at that time.

While smoking a cigarette he went out to the garden and as he threw away the stub he noticed a handsome young man seated there.

'Why are you seated here?' Ashok asked. 'What do you want?'

The young man stood up and said, 'Sir, my name is Dev Anand. I am an actor, and I want a job.'

'Have you acted before?' Ashok quizzed him. 'Are you acting in any film right now?'

'I acted in one film which did not do well,' Dev Anand informed him. 'I have no work now.'

Ashok looked at the young man with sympathy and said,

'Come with me.' He took him to Shahid Latif and said, 'Shahid, please meet this young man, he may answer your requirement.'

Shahid said, 'I'll see.'

Ashok went back to his room. Soon Shahid, Ismat and Manto trooped in. 'Dadamoni,' Shahid said, 'I insist that you do the role.'

Manto said, 'Yes Dadamoni, this role has been tailored for you and you alone.'

Ashok said, 'Don't think about me but tell me, does the young man suit your requirement to the maximum?' Shahid shook his head. 'No, Dadamoni, he looks like a chocolate bar.' The other two repeated the word 'chocolate' to convey that the young man was handsome, yes, but expressionless.

Ashok said, 'No, I don't agree. He is not as much of a chocolate as I was. You have to work with him.'

The three became vociferous and argued on, but Ashok was adamant. 'No,' he said, 'I am not mentally fit to act now. Let that chap Dev Anand do the role, I will stand behind him.' That was the last word and Dev Anand was taken up as the hero in *Ziddi*, made in 1948.

This film did not fare well at the box office. But it did one thing: it initiated Kishore Kumar into film music. He sang all the songs in the film.

Ashok Kumar is fond of ghost stories and he would often question: Do ghosts exist? One day some workers reported that some of them had watched the ghost of Himanshu Rai stalk the compound after midnight, in his white shirt and pants and carrying a tin of cigarettes in his hand.

Ashok told them, 'Call me the moment you spot the ghost again.'

That night people from the sets department again saw the vision and came running to Ashok Kumar.

Ashok hurried but by the time he reached the ghost had vanished. He sat there and started to wonder: How can anyone see a ghost? Perhaps one can. Perhaps ghosts do exist. Himanshu Rai founded this institution, he loved it, he died while working for it— that may be why, perhaps...

Then it struck him. There was the art director Tagore, who dressed in a style reminiscent of Himanshu Rai and with the same habit of walking into the night!

'Call Tagore,' he sent off someone.

Tagore was going to bed when he was summoned. Ashok asked, 'Tagore, why do you scare people?'

'Do I?' Tagore wondered. 'How could you say that, Dadamoni!'

Ashok said in a stern voice, 'You smoke regularly?'

'Yes, I do.'

'What brand?'

'Gold Flake.'

'Do you carry the packet in your hand?'

'I prefer it from a tin but yes, I carry it in my hand.'

'You hold the tin behind your back?'

'That's right.'

'And you walk around the studio premises?'

'Yes, I've to keep late hours to inspect the progress of the set erection. Moreover, I like to stroll around.'

'And you prefer white shirts and trousers?'

Tagore smiled, 'You are right. You can call me "The Man in White". But why this interrogation? You are behaving like a CID Inspector, Dadamoni!'

Ashok smiled. 'And you are the supposed ghost of Himanshu Rai.'

When he narrated the belief of the workers to Tagore, they all had a hearty laugh. So, Tagore was the 'ghost' of Rai.

But the thought kept haunting Ashok Kumar. Why do people talk of ghosts? Do they really exist?

A month later Ashok Kumar's wife (yes, he was married! He got married in 1938) Shobha had gone to Pune and Ashok thought of holidaying for two days and went to Khandala where she would join him. But no bungalow was available, except for Jeejeebhoy House which was not hired by anyone as it was said to be haunted.

Ashok did not feel scared. On the contrary, he felt challenged. Do ghosts really exist? This was his chance to find out.

It was past midnight. The servant had gone out to meet some friends. Ashok heard some raised voices and going to the gate found a lady quarrelling with her driver near her car. The lady was fair-looking and when she saw Ashok she said she needed water for the car.

'Why not?' Ashok said. 'You are welcome.'

The lady came to the verandah of the house with the driver and after Ashok gave her a bottle of water, she instructed the driver to set the car right. The driver went away and the lady sat there and waited. Ashok offered her whisky which she politely refused.

The driver returned shortly to say that nothing can be done, they would have to get another vehicle. They left the car right there and walked away.

Ashok locked the door and since the house was haunted, he drank himself to sleep. Much later at night he woke up. Someone was calling: 'Sahib! O Sahib! Sahib!'

Ashok felt compelled to go out, for it sounded like a man in distress. But he found no one at the gate although the call was repeated. So he walked towards the car which was still outside the gate. Looking in he was shocked to see a man there, his throat slit, breathing his last. Oh God!

Next morning Ashok woke up with the nightmare still fresh in his mind. He called his servant and said, 'A horrible thing happened last night. A man has been murdered in the car right outside our house.'

'But that cannot be true, sir,' the servant said. 'There's no car there.'

Ashok was not convinced. He went to the Police Station and reported the incident. The inspector heard him out and then asked, 'Are you staying at the Jeejeebhoy House?'

'Yes,' Ashok replied.

'This murder took place exactly fourteen years ago,' the inspector said. 'A woman murdered someone and fled. Then she died in a car accident.'

Ashok could only stare at the inspector.

Returning to Malad, Ashok narrated this experience to some people. One day Kamal Amrohi came out with a story which ran like this: Shankar, the son of an eminent judge, comes to live in Sangam Bhavan, a haunted palace bought by his father. He is met by the old gardener and his daughter, Asha.

Shankar is determined to unravel the mystery surrounding the house which has been lying vacant for the last forty years. The story goes that the king who had built the palace for his beloved consort was murdered on their wedding night. Ever since, the queen's spirit has haunted the deserted mansion.

Shankar is shocked when he stumbles upon the portrait of a man who looked exactly like him. Soon enough he meets the queen, feels an irresistible attraction for her and starts believing that he is the reincarnation of the king. His friend Sreenath's effort to deflect the obsession fails but ultimately, Shankar is married to Ranjana, his fiancée. Yet the bond with the spirit holds and the marriage remains unconsummated. When a heartbroken Ranjana commits suicide, Shankar is accused of murder.

During the trial Asha, confesses that she acted as the spirit in order to make Shankar fall in love with her. In spite of Sreenath's efforts, Shankar is sentenced to death. Shankar, while parting, importunes his friend to marry Asha to break the spell cast upon their love, maybe he will be united with Asha in their next lives. But an evidence saves Shankar at the last minute and when he arrives at the palace, Sreenath is already married to Asha. Shankar had come only to die.

The story was liked by all. Ashok agreed to act and after a good deal of search cast the honey-faced Madhubala. Wirsching had returned by then and wielded the camera. The music scored by Khemchand Prakash was all melody and haunted the listeners. It was a rare music which lifted the viewers and listeners to a mysterious, unearthly world. People would play the record late into the night and savour the eerie sadness, particularly of the most popular number, '*Ayega, ayega, ayega aanewala, ayega-a-a.*'

The name of the playback singer, Lata Mangeshkar, became a household word after *Mahal*. The film was equally successful. And Ashok Kumar's performance reached another high point. He was brilliant as the obsessed and haunted lover.

Nitin Bose is a shining name in the annals of Indian cinema. He had made classics at New Theatres and was considered a superb technician who had rendered some pioneering service to the Indian film craft.

Ashok invited Nitin Bose to make films for Bombay Talkies, and *Samar* was made in 1949.

Next year Nitin Bose made *Mashal*. This time Ashok acted opposite Sumitra Devi of New Theatres fame and Ruma Devi, a niece of Satyajit Ray who was to later become Kishore Kumar's first wife. Sachin Dev Burman had scored the music for Filmistan's *Shikari* but three years had passed since and he was unable to make a place for himself in Bombay. He decided to go back to Bengal and came to say goodbye to Ashok. 'Score the music for *Mashal* and then go back,' Ashok said to him. S.D. Burman scored the music and the songs of *Mashal* became so popular that Bombay made him a prisoner for life.

Aravind Sen, a new director, made *Muqaddar* starring a new face, Nalini Jaywant. Ashok Kumar then assigned the direction of *Tamasha* to Phani Mazumdar, another renowned director of

New Theatres who had made major Bengali hits like *Street Singer*, *Kapal Kundala*, *Sapera* and *Doctor*. Mazumdar's *Tamasha* paired upcoming actress Meena Kumari with Dev Anand.

Ashok now invited Bimal Roy from Calcutta. Roy was then the craze of Bengali cinegoers for his *Udayer Pathey*. That was the first super hit after *Chandidas*. *Udayer Pathey* introduced social realism and the clash of capitalism and trade unionism. The film made its mark in its Hindi version *Humrahi* as well by its masterly handling of story, situations, dialogue and performances. Moreover, every film of his was cinematographically brilliant since at base he was a cameraman. Before leaving Calcutta, he had made *Anjangarh* and *Pahela Aadmi*, honouring Netaji's INA.

Bimal Roy came down with his crew and made *Maa*, starring Bharat Bhushan and Shyama. The film became a silver-jubilee hit.

In 1950, Ashok Kumar invited Gyan Mukherjee of *Kismet* fame to make a film. This time the two of them planned something unusual. Going off the trodden path, Ashok Kumar was to play a negative role which would be a contrast to the goody-goody roles he had done so far.

In the past when Himanshu Rai was alive, Ashok used to express his desire to try his hand at comedy. Himanshu Rai would shake his head and say, 'No Ashok, never do comic roles. Always accept straight, serious roles, positive roles.'

There was logic behind what he said. For, there is a difference between the stage and the screen. Onstage the illusion of reality is never total. As such, no matter how powerful the emotional impact, the performance factor is what remains supreme in the subconscious of the viewer. He accepts the ability of the actor and remembers him for that. So the actor can, like Sisir Bhaduri of the Bengali stage did, perform as Rama one night and the next night play the role of Alamgir Aurangzeb, the Mughal emperor—a diametrically opposite character.

On the other hand, in films, because of the total illusion of reality, the spectator's identification with the actor is supreme.

He starts to sympathise with him and even idolise him. The hero or heroine merges with the individual's ideal of male or female. Else, they learn to define and formulate their idols, heroes and heroines. As a result, film heroes and heroines become the object of love and adoration, at time helping the viewers to channelise their repressed sexual fantasies. That is proved by the fact that normally audiences do not like their heroes and heroines to marry, for everywhere in the world virginity is prized.

Himanshu Rai did not talk about any negative role. And what is a negative role? It is a role where a character does wrong things, things prohibited by society or law. He or she does the opposite of what is done by the positive characters.

The story that Gyan Mukherjee and Ashok Kumar evolved this time unfolded around a totally negative character. The hero, a handsome young man, was the son of an honest police officer but had gone to dogs because, following his mother's death in his childhood, he was pampered to the extreme. He would lie to his father and exploit his love, he would raid bars and extract money to gamble in dens of inequity. He loved a girl whom he forcibly lifted from the marriage pandal as she was being given away to the bridegroom. He finally murdered her, kissed the revolver and shot down the policemen who had come to arrest him. In the finale he was shot down by his own father. Every bit about the character was negative.

Ashok knew his audience loved him, adored him, idealised and even idolised him. Yet the artiste in him felt challenged to play this role to prove his artistic range. The man who had once hated the thought of acting was by now in love with acting, having tasted the joy, the rasa of merging with a concept, a character.

He acted as the hero and the object of his love and passion, the girl, was to be played by Nalini Jaywant. This was their first pairing. The film was titled *Sangram*. The actor who played the role of Ashok as a child was none other than Shashi Kapoor, then aged only fourteen. He was treated as a child when the picture was completed, as it was labelled 'For Adults Only' by the Censor Board, and poor Shashi could not see his own performance in his first film. The actress who played the role of Nalini as a child? She was Baby Tabassum, the top star amongst the child artistes at that time.

Sangram was the first of its kind—a well-crafted mixture of sex and violence. It was perhaps the first film on the life of an angry young man which seems to be the modern trend.

Sangram became a hit. All the houses showing it were continuously 'Full' for sixteen weeks. People used to joke with police constables on the streets and say, 'Go and see *Sangram*, see how Ashok Kumar has taken you to task.'

Police officers felt piqued and reported this to the then chief minister of Maharashtra, Mr Morarji Desai.

Morarji called Ashok Kumar, 'You have to do two things, Mr Ashok Kumar. First, you have to withdraw your film from the cinema houses, and this you must do by tomorrow. The second, is my request to you—play the role of an honest police inspector.'

Sangram was thus banned in Maharashtra after the sixteenth week. Ashok Kumar did not protest, he felt happy that the audience had accepted him in a negative role and he felt that he had laid bare another dimension of his acting capability.

Gyan Mukherjee was a clever director who knew that the audience would not hate the hero due to the emotional trauma suffered by him at the loss of his mother. Apart from this, the story proved his unusual love for the heroine.

In retrospect, Ashok Kumar would say with a naughty smile and a twinkle in his eyes, 'No matter how negative the role was, my female fans liked me very much for it.'

After he took over Bombay Talkies, for three years between 1947 and 1949, Ashok Kumar did not accept any outside film roles. Nor did he act in all the productions of his unit despite the fact that he was the most popular hero of the day and producers were constantly chasing him. The reason lay in his basic character. He was serious about anything he took up. During those three years, his ambition was to breathe life into the flagging institution, Bombay Talkies. He invited the best directors, artistes, writers and the best music directors to work for it. His love for the institution percolated down to all the workers of the concern. Everyone used to stay at Malad, and considered one another as members of one big family. Ashok, during that period, did not seek anything for himself. Whatever he did, was all for his love, Bombay Talkies. He used to write scenes, discuss, sit in at editing, listen to music, explain scenes by demonstrating to artistes how to act but never hankered after credit for all he did.

At that time he was perhaps unconsciously seized with the ambition of playing God.

Everything is temporal. Even an institution.

Majboor, Ziddi, Mahal, Muqaddar, Mashal, Tamasha, Sangram, Maa—most of these films ran to packed houses and earned good money. But the outstanding Rs 3 lakh were still unpaid! Did that mean that no profit had been earned after all these films? They sat down with all the account books and Ashok detected corruption and shameless dishonesty.

The accountant had procured Ashok's signature on blank papers and removed huge sums. Besides many other discrepancies, it was found that even handsome allowances were remitted every month to someone's mistress!

Ashok felt outraged. Out of disgust he started to pay off the outstanding sum out of his own pocket. He sold off his shares at throwaway prices and bid adieu to his love, Bombay Talkies, in 1953.

Those who took control of Bombay Talkies felt, after some time, that they were neither fit nor imaginative enough to run the concern. They lost interest and Bombay Talkies went into liquidation. Life moved on to the next page in the annals of

Indian cinema. For, everything that is born under the sun must die. Even institutions.

Some years back a man went to interview Ashok Kumar. He said, 'You say Bombay Talkies has come to an end? I say Bombay Talkies is still continuing, Dadamoni.'

'How do you say that?' Ashok Kumar queried. The man replied, 'Because you are Bombay Talkies. And you are here.'

Ashok Kumar said, 'No, I am not. Come with me, I will show you Bombay Talkies.'

He led the man from his room upstairs to the drawing room on the ground floor and respectfully pointed to the garlanded bust of Himanshu Rai. 'Only he and no one else is Bombay Talkies. He made me what I am today.'

CHAPTER 11

FROM A RIVER UNTO THE SEA

Change is the law that rules the universe. Nothing is perpetual, nothing remains the same. The studio system of yesteryears sounds like an improbable fairy tale now.

Changes followed the Independence days. All the film concerns turned towards escapist fare and only escapist fare. The serious edge got blurred. All love for ideals came to an end with the achievement of Independence. The accent was on making it big by striking rich. Producers were less concerned with quality and more with buying Cadillacs and diamonds. Everyone has a right to earn big money but they were in extra haste and that is a sort of sin.

In this changing atmosphere Ashok Kumar once again turned towards acting.

In early 1951, a man started to come to Ashok. He came repeatedly for some days but Ashok had no time for him. One day he thought of disposing of the man and asked, 'What can I do for you, sir?'

The man humbly replied, 'I have a script with me, it has a double role for you. I shall be grateful if you agree to do that.'

Ashok asked, 'Who are you? What do you do?'

'I was a journalist,' the man answered. 'I have come to Bombay as a refugee after the Partition. I need your help.'

Ashok felt the man was too demanding. 'You have never learnt the film craft, then how can you aspire to make one?' he asked. 'I am an actor now but after learning the craft as a technician. And you want to make it by writing a single script. Please take some other actor.'

The man went away in silence. But after a few days he reappeared carrying letters of recommendation from various friends and producers.

Ashok contained his vexation with the thought that the man, being a refugee, was desperate. He agreed to work for him.

On the first day of shooting Ashok found a crowd of journalists, almost forty of them, talking loudly and guffawing. Annoyed, Ashok said to the director, 'I can't work in such an atmosphere.'

'Please manage upto lunch, sir,' the man requested. 'From tomorrow none shall come.'

After the first shot was taken the man came to Ashok and said, 'Sir, I had conceived the action differently. I mean your action...' he did not complete his sentence.

Ashok almost lost his composure, but said slowly, 'I can, of course, act according to your suggestion but the scene will get out of tune. Don't blame me then.'

The man kept up and said, 'But I thought otherwise. Well, it is all right then because you are saying. No more takes.'

But Ashok normally honours others' opinions and suggestions, for he believes that there is no end to learning. So he said, 'No, I will now give a take according to your thought. Develop both the takes tonight so that I can see them at 8 a.m. tomorrow. If my shot seems right, then you will let me work according to my reasoning and never bother me in future.'

The man politely agreed.

Next morning, exactly at 8 a.m. both the shots were projected. Ashok found that the mood of the moment was better interpreted by the director.

'What is your full name?' he asked the young man, 'I have forgotten.'

'Baldev Rao Chopra,' the man shyly replied.

Ashok gravely continued, 'What does your father call you?'

'Baldev,' he answered.

Ashok stretched out his hand and caught hold of Chopra's. 'From now on, I will also address you like your father. Baldev, you were right, I didn't perceive the scene correctly.'

That was the start of a special relationship between B.R. Chopra and Ashok Kumar. That particular film was *Afasana*, based on a story by I.S. Johar, a writer who was also an actor. The cameraman was Rajendra Malone and the cast headed by Ashok Kumar included Veena, Kuldip Kaur and Pran.

Afasana is the story of twin brothers Chaman and Ratan who get separated in a village fair during a storm. Ratan loses his memory and is brought up in an orphanage as Ashok. He works his way up to become a magistrate, is loved and respected by all, and is married to Leela (Kuldip Kaur).

Meanwhile Chaman inherits his father's wealth, has become a theatre magnate and developed the arrogance of the rich. The only soft spot is his love for their childhood playmate Meera (Veena) who herself loves the other twin.

Wrongly implicated in a case of murder, Chaman escapes to Mussoorie where he meets his lookalike. In order to escape from the hands of the law, he impersonates as Ratan and escapes—only to die in an accident, thus 'killing' Ashok.

Meanwhile, a drugged Ashok wakes up to find he is no longer bearded and no longer Ashok. It suits him to be Chaman, however, since he is disillusioned with his wife who is having an affair with his friend. Soon he is also free under the law as the case against Chaman is withdrawn.

Ashok—originally Ratan and now forced to be Chaman—takes stock of his new surroundings. He is cured of his amnesia with the help of Meera who recognises him by the scar on his chest. His wife commits suicide, his 'friend' is ruined and dies too. Ratan is free to start a new life.

Afsana was a big hit of 1951. Ashok Kumar gave an extremely good account, as per the press and the public, in the twin role of Chaman and Ashok. Though the story was old wine, the film had enough dramatic value, and well portrayed on the screen it became a big success with the masses.

In *Afsana* B.R. Chopra showed plenty of enterprise and understanding. It started his climb up the ladder of success, making one good film after another till he reached the epic *Mahabharat*. He is deservedly one of the most important men in the Hindi film industry.

In his next film *Sholay* (1953), Ashok was cast against the fair beauty Bina Rai. It was a mediocre film but the one that came next, in 1956, was a hit: *Ek Hi Rasta*, with Meena Kumari and Sunil Dutt. In 1960 he again worked with Chopra in his *Kanoon*, where his co-stars were Rajendra Kumar and Nanda. Ashok immensely enjoyed working in this film, a tale of how the law can send an innocent man to the gallows.

Young public prosecutor Kailash Khanna is engaged to Meena, Judge Badri Prasad's collegiate daughter. Her brother Vijay is a wastrel, squandering money on girls and clubs. His indiscriminate borrowings from moneylender Dhaniram lands him into trouble. Dhaniram holds a blank paper with the brother's signature— and at Meera's request Kailash makes a nocturnal trip to the moneylender's house to get back the document. There, to his horror, he witnesses the murder of Dhaniram!

The morning papers report the arrest of a petty thief for the murder. When the case comes up in court, Kailash decides to defend the thief, as he believes in fighting for the truth even at the cost of his love, honour or indeed his own life. As the trial progresses, the mystery deepens, building up to an unexpected climax...

Ashok Kumar, playing the judge, gave a brilliant performance and B.R. Chopra was lauded for his courage to take up such a theme. Not only that: Chopra proved that a film can be popular even without a song. Ashok Kumar and the rest of the troupe kept the audience spellbound by their performance.

In *Kanoon* once again Ashok Kumar proved his artistic zeal and sincerity, his dedication for achieving perfection. For this role, he made several trips to the courts to watch the cross examinations. He used as his prototype the renowned Justice Chagla.

Kanoon was a hit. So was *Gumraah*, the next film he did for B.R. Chopra. Cast against Mala Sinha and Sunil Dutt, he gave a sterling performance as the loving husband who kept a watch over his wife and steered her back from the verge of infidelity.

Deedar was another successful film made in 1951, the same year as *Afsana*. It was directed by Nitin Bose. Ashok Kumar co-starred with Nargis and Dilip Kumar.

Between 1947 and 1949, when Ashok did not take up any outside offer as he was busy reconstructing Bombay Talkies, new heroes had entered the scene. Three of them had specially made a mark: Dilip Kumar, Raj Kapoor and Dev Anand. Two films produced and directed by Raj Kapoor—*Aag* (1948) and *Barsaat* (1949)—were liked by viewers. *Barsaat* was in fact a super hit. Suddenly Ashok Kumar became conscious that he cannot neglect his acting career and help people to forget him so soon. He started to welcome offers and as a result nine films featuring him released in 1952—and all of them had successful runs. These were *Betaab, Bewafa, Jalpari, Kafila, Nau Bahar, Poonam, Raag Rang, Saloni* and *Tamasha*.

His fears were unfounded—the audience adored him just as they did before.

Ashok produced jointly with one Mr Kapoor a memorable film, *Parineeta*. Based on a novelette by Saratchandra, it was directed by Bimal Roy. It was a charming, powerful film which had, for its dominant element, a tender romance unfolding amidst an acrid drama of religious inflexibility. Set in an atmosphere of Hindu middle-class domesticity, it portrayed a group of familiar, close to life characters in the normal course of living their everyday life.

The narrative unfolded around Lalita, the orphaned niece of a poor but honest clerk, Gurucharan. She has an informal but close relationship with Shekhar, the younger son of Navinchandra, their neighbouring landlord. Gurucharan's hereditary house is mortgaged to Navin and because he cannot clear his debt the friendship between the families is threatened.

Girin, an educated young man who is visiting his sister in the house nextdoor, comes to Gurucharan's rescue with an interest-free loan. And Gurucharan finds enough courage to challenge the autocratic Navinchandra and his Brahmin cronies.

Girin is attracted towards Lalita. This upsets Shekhar, who realises he had taken Lalita to be so much a part of his life and surroundings that he was never conscious of his possessive love for her.

After many ups and downs in the relationships, on the very day of his wedding to someone else, Shekhar gathers the courage to declare to the world that he and Lalita are in love and are secretly married.

Excellent direction and superb portrayals by Ashok Kumar, Meena Kumari and the other artistes invested *Parineeta* with a life that holds to this day, belying the four decades that have gone by.

After *Parineeta*, Ashok Kumar worked in two more films for Bimal Roy Productions. The second, *Bandini*, came almost ten years later. It had a unique story.

Kalyani, an attractive young woman convicted for murder, comes to the notice of the paternal jailer for her quiet and reserved personality. The handsome young prison doctor falls in love with her even though she does not reciprocate. As a result of the whispers that spread through the prison grapevine, and disheartened by lack of response from Kalyani, the doctor resigns and leaves.

The jailer wonders at the girl's reluctance to marry the doctor and wants to know the reason. Kalyani writes down her story and submits it to the jailer, and her past unfolds.

The struggle for freedom was at its height. Bikash, a political detenu, was detained in a village. Guarded round the clock by the police, he was allowed to talk to only the government employees. So Bikash starts to visit the village postmaster, and there meets his daughter, Kalyani.

Bikash and Kalyani are drawn to each other and through many dramatic moments arrive at a situation where Bikash, running a high temperature, is discovered by the police sleeping in Kalyani's bedroom. To salvage the situation, Bikash declares his love for Kalyani and his resolve to marry her as soon as he is released.

Thereafter Bikash is led away from the village to the city for trial and is eventually released. But he does not return to marry Kalyani and the village society is rocked by scandals that start hounding the postmaster. To relieve her father of the torture, Kalyani leaves for the city, where she finds a job as an attendant in a nursing home. Here she comes face to face with Bikash, whose wife, a mentally demented sadistic woman, is a patient. In a moment of emotional imbalance, feeling betrayed by Bikash, she poisons the tea she was carrying for the wife. The patient dies and Kalyani lands in jail.

The jailer is moved by Kalyani's story, and persuades Kalyani to marry the doctor who is still waiting for her.

Kalyani, because of her exemplary behaviour, gets an early reprieve and the jailer sends her with a female warden to the doctor's town.

The train arrives at a junction on the banks of Ganga from where the steamer takes people to destinations across the river. There, while waiting for her train, Kalyani meets Bikash, now a sick man with pulmonary disease, being escorted to his native village by two young activists of his party. From them she learns that Bikash was a political activist of exemplary integrity and nationalistic spirit. He loved someone but could not keep his word to her because the party insisted that he marry the only sister of a martyred party member. Bikash had made the supreme sacrifice in spite of his deep love.

When Bikash saw Kalyani, he begged her pardon and wishing her happiness left for the steamer with the young man without divulging to her his predicament.

The train was setting in motion when Kalyani heard the siren of the steamer. All at once she got off the moving train and ran towards the ghat where the ship was lifting anchor, made her way to the deck where Bikash was seated and fell at his feet. She had reached her love, for good.

When Bimal Roy approached Ashok Kumar to play the role of Bikash, he did not respond immediately for he had a vague feeling of dissatisfaction about the hero's betrayal. But when he heard stories about the sacrifices of the pre-Independence revolutionaries and particularly about the difficult and all-demanding party discipline, he agreed to do the role. He also agreed to the compliment Roy paid to him: 'Dadamoni, there is none else who can laugh heartily like you in the role of Bikash.' And Ashok Kumar laughed the laughter of Bikash.

Once again, brilliant direction and excellent performances by Nutan, Dharmendra and Tarun Bose and above all Ashok Kumar, embellished with S.D. Burman's soul-stirring melodies, gave *Bandini* a classic dimension. It was hailed as a cinematic experience by all who saw it.

The other film Ashok did for Bimal Roy was *Benazir*. It was not directed by Roy but by a little known technician, S. Khalil. It failed to make any impression, but Ashok Kumar did.

Actors and actresses travel to faraway places in the world for shooting. Ashok Kumar once flew to Egypt in 1953. The shooting was done mostly in Cairo. The film was *Naaz*, the glamorous

Nalini Jaywant was the heroine, the director was S.K. Ojha. The film, released in 1954, was a very mediocre one.

However, the same year an excellent film was made by Phani Mazumdar. Produced by the Bombay Talkies Workers Cooperative Society, it was one of the few multistarrers of its time: it featured Ashok Kumar, Dev Anand, Meena Kumari and Usha Kiran amongst a host of artistes who had worked in Bombay Talkies films. The music was composed by Timir Baran, the world-renowned composer of Uday Shankar Ballet group, and Hemant Kumar's golden voice was used to such advantage that it secured him a permanent place in Bombay.

The film depicted the lives of fisherfolks on the Maharashtra seacoast and Ashok Kumar gave a memorable performance. But due to a conflict among the workers, *Baadbaan* could not exploit these advantages. And the latest on the film is that its negative is damaged beyond rescue.

In the early 1960s, Ashok gave up his own production, for it seemed a headache more than anything else. His company had produced *Raagini*, *Kalpana* and *Meri Soorat Teri Aankhen*, all mediocre fares, and then he was always weak on business: people he had trusted had been cheating him. His secretary got his signature on a paper and Ashok was trapped. He quit as a producer and concentrated only on acting.

Ashok Kumar has been in films for fifty-six years now, and has acted in more than 300 films. About 250 films were flops or forgettable but at least fifty were superhits, or of exceptional artistic merit.

These fifty films have been directed by various film-makers. We have already mentioned some of them, like Franz Osten, Gyan Mukherjee, N.R. Acharya, Kamal Amrohi, Nitin Bose, Phani Mazumdar, B.R. Chopra and Bimal Roy. Among the others were the following.

Devaki Bose is a highly regarded name in Indian cinema, particularly of Bengal. Ashok was impressed by his films while he was studying law in Calcutta. *Puran Bhagat*, *Chandidas*, *Vidyapati* are still cherished by people. Bose won the National award for the brilliant *Sagar Sangamey*, an emotional experience in Bengali. As a man Devaki Bose was learned as well as deeply religious.

In 1947 Bose called Ashok to play a role in the Bankim Chandra classic, *Chandrasekhar*, a stirring tale set against the Mutiny, and offered him Rs 2.5 lakh. The most glamorous heroine of the time, the golden-voiced Kanan Devi, was cast opposite him. The film in Bengali was extremely popular.

Another Bengali film starring Ashok Kumar was released in 1960. The heroine was Suchitra Sen, a glamorous name of the Indian screen. Ashok played the role of a house surgeon in love with his colleague, the surgeon played by Suchitra. The film, *Hospital*, was directed by the veteran director Sushil Mazumdar who had an excellent sense of acting.

Ashok Kumar is an admirer of Tapan Sinha. The director has made many Bengali and some Hindi films, and all of them have a distinctive air about them. Among his most distinguished films are *Kshudhita Pashan* (Hungry Stones), *Kabuliwala* and *Atithi*—all based on Tagore's stories—in Bengali and *Sagina Mahato* and *Ek Doctor Ki Maut* in Hindi.

A rare craftsman and an excellent technician, Tapan Sinha is an adept screenwriter. Above all, he is a very sensitive director. He was responsible for Ashok Kumar's third Bengali film, *Haatey Bajarey*. Based on a novel by Banaphool (one of the many giants of Bengali literature, better known for his *Bhuvan Shome* though it was made much later), the film grows around an idealistic doctor (played by Ashok Kumar). Living in a small town cradled by hills, he is always ready to help the poor and the distressed. His wife's ill health is a constant agony to him.

The town and the outskirts are terrorised by the arrogant son of the local zamindar, Lachman, who harasses and molests the village women.

One day Lachman's roving eyes settle upon Chhipli, a beautiful young widow. His advances to her are thwarted by the avuncular doctor. After his wife's death the doctor opens a medical service unit with the help of Chhipli—now a nurse—a retired sub judge and a young doctor from Calcutta.

But the peace does not last. The doctor is attacked by a lackey of Lachman. Good strikes back at the evil—the doctor strangles Lachman but is himself mortally wounded.

The brilliant treatment and direction, along with the music, by Tapan Sinha, ably assisted by the cameraman Dinen Gupta and the performances of Vyjayantimala (Chhipli), Ajitesh Banerjee (Lachman) and above all Ashok Kumar, combined to make *Haatey Bajarey* a most memorable film.

Ashok acted in *Bandish* directed by Satyen Bose in 1955—the film was a hit and had a different kind of story that was based on *Chheley Kaar* (Whose Son?) by Jyotirmoy Roy, the renowned story writer of Bimal Roy's *Udayer Pathey*.

The orphaned Tomato is brought up by Mahendra who, suffering from tuberculosis, plants the child on a young man Kamal, deemed a suitable guardian among those in the park that day. Tomato is convinced that Kamal is really his long-lost father.

Kamal feels attracted towards the child but he has his own problems and does not take the child seriously. But Tomato does not give up easily and clings tightly to his 'Papa'. This results in many embarrassing situations. But the quick-witted Tomato (Daisy Irani) soon wins the hearts of 'Papa' Kamal (Ashok Kumar) and 'Mummy' Usha, Kamal's girlfriend (Meena Kumari)—and everyone is happy.

The film turned out to be a rollicking comedy of errors, one of the best of its kind on the Indian screen in years. The comedy was not laboured, crude or artificial. It was simply glorious entertainment.

In 1956 Ashok acted in Satyen Bose's *Bandi* but the major kudos went to his brother Kishore Kumar.

Satyen Bose as a director had a flair for comedy. *Bandish* proved that, and in 1958 it was proved once again with *Chalti Ka Naam Gaadi*, another comedy non pareil. The film had all the three brothers—Ashok, Anoop and Kishore Kumar—in it with Veena and Madhubala in the female leads. The music by S.D. Burman added exceedingly to the film's comic spirit. It was a unique blend which stands apart, to this day, from the so-called comedies on the Indian screen.

Ashok Kumar proved his histrionic range by handling the comic situations with as much ease as he showed in the emotion-charged moments.

Enjoying a good rapport with Satyen Bose, he also acted in *Savera* (1958), *Sitaron Se Aagey* (1958), *Masoom* (1960), *Aansoo Ban Gaye Phool*—based on Marathi playwright Vasant Kanetkar's *Ashrunchi Jhali Phoole* (1968)—*Sa-Re-Ga-Ma-Pa* (1972) and *Mastan Dada* (1977).

Once, in the early Bombay Talkies years, when Ashok happened to mention his desire to try his hand at comedy, Himanshu Rai shook his head in disapproval. 'No Ashok, never do comic roles. Do straight roles, serious roles, they suit you better.' But Ashok later proved—amply at that—that he can be natural and convincing even when doing comic roles.

'I inherited the flair for comedy from my father,' Ashok once said. 'Though he never acted in his whole life, he was quite a comedian. As an advocate, whenever he cross-examined a witness, the accused laughed, the plaintiff laughed, the other advocates laughed and the judge laughed too. The whole court would resound with laughter and more laughter.'

He had further said, 'Amongst all three of us, Kishore inherited this way with the funny stuff from our father, for he was the dearest pet, being the youngest. On returning home from the court, Father would go out carrying Kishore on his shoulder, Kishore's feet dangling on both sides. While father walked, Kishore would use his bald pate to play the tabla!'

This flair for comedy was well exploited by director Brij in *Victoria No. 203*. Ashok had been a favourite star of Brij since 1959 and by 1975 he had made seven films with him. These include *Nai Rahen* with Geeta Bali (1959), *Ustadon Ke Ustad* with Pradeep Kumar and Shakila (1963), *Afsana* with Pradeep Kumar and Padmini (1966), *Do Bhai* with Mala Sinha and Jeetendra (1969), *Victoria No. 203* with Saira Banu, Navin Nischol and Pran (1972), *Paise Ki Gudiya* with Navin Nischol and Saira Banu (1974) and *Chori Mera Kaam* with Shashi Kapoor and Zeenat Aman (1975).

Ashok attaches significance to only two of these, *Do Bhai* and, in particular, *Victoria No. 203*. In this film he and Pran formed a delightful pair, and proved beyond a spec of doubt the class he belonged to as an actor. A smile automatically plays on your lips whenever you hum the song rendered by the duo in *Victoria No. 203*: 'Do bechaare, bina sahaare, dekho puchh puchh kar hare... / Bin taley ki chaabi lekar phirte maare mare...'

Basu Chatterjee, a leading name among the Indian 'New Wave' directors, took full advantage of Ashok Kumar's comic genius in *Chhoti Si Baat*. The wonderful set up of the film was provided by B.R. Chopra, by this time a 'grand moghul' of Indian films. He put K.K. Mahajan behind the camera, gave the baton to Salil Chowdhury, and cast Amol Palekar and Vidya Sinha in the romantic leads.

Ashok Kumar was Col J.N.W. Singh, an old scoundrel who gives a crash course to the shy, diffident Amol on how to win Vidya Sinha. This fizzy romantic comedy was inspired by the British comedy *School for Scandal*. The highly successful film established Basu Chatterjee as a sound bet at the box-office.

Basu's next film *Khatta Meetha* again had Ashok Kumar. He portrayed a middle-aged Parsi who marries a lady of equal age—

played by Pearl Padamsee—both with three children each from their earlier marriages. Both were delightful. Ashok continued to delight in Basu's later films, *Safed Jhooth* (1977), *Tumhare Liye* and *Shaukeen* in particular.

Shaukeen and *Khatta Meetha* are the two Ashok enjoyed doing, he says.

In 1964, Ashok did a different kind of role in *Chitralekha* directed by Kidar Sharma. The story of a monk in love with a courtesan was set in a period 2000 years back in time.

Then, in 1967, he acted as a villain in Dev Anand's *Jewel Thief*, under Vijay Anand's direction.

He acted in several films directed by the well-known director from the south, A. Bhim Singh. Of these *Raakhi* has been the most successful. Ashok played the brother who made utmost sacrifices to ensure the happiness of his sister, Waheeda Rehman. Its release in 1962 was followed by *Pooja Ke Phool* (1964), *Meherban* (1967), *Bhai Behen* (1969) and *Malik* (1972).

With Asit Sen of Calcutta (distinct from the comedian Asit Sen who also began as a director) Ashok acted in three films: *Mamta* (1966), which as *Uttar Phalguni* had been a hit in Bengali too, then *Safar* which was a remake of *Chalachal*, and *Sharafat*—all of which were big hits with the audience.

Eighteen years after *Baadbaan* was made in 1954, Ashok did a second film with Phani Mazumdar. *Aarti*, this time, was a hit. It was followed by *Akash Deep* and *Oonchey Log*, both in 1965. In both these films Ashok had meaty roles and he did justice to them. But neither of these two had more than a mediocre response at the box office.

Producer director Shakti Samanta, a big name in Hindi films, had started out as assistant to Phani Mazumdar. He directed his first film with Ashok Kumar as *Inspector* (1956), and *Sheroo* (1957).

Both the films did well enough to establish Samanta's valuation at the box office. Then came *Howrah Bridge* (1958), starring Ashok Kumar and Madhubala, with music by O.P. Nayyar, the most popular music director at the time. It was a big hit.

Anuraag (1972) was another film Ashok did for Samanta. Then came *Anand Aashram*, a remake of the Bengali *Doctor*, the emotion-charged superhit his guru Phani Mazumdar had done for New Theatres. It co-starred Ashok with Uttam Kumar, the legend of Bengal, and Sharmila Tagore. Both the films were, of course, major hits.

Ashok Kumar holds Hrishikesh Mukherjee in high esteem as a director. Hrishi came to Bombay with Bimal Roy in 1951, as his editor. A brilliant technician, he charted out an independent course as a director after *Do Bigha Zameen*, right in 1954. In 1968 he approached Ashok with a role.

'Dadamoni,' he said, 'here's a role that will fetch you an award.'

'I'm not tempted by awards, Hrishi,' Ashok had said, 'but I am by roles. So tell me the story.'

And Hrishi narrated: 'Set against a feudalistic background, it is the story of a zamindar's son-in-law who pits himself against injustice and cruelty. The consequences are tragic.'

Shivnath Chowdhury, the middle-aged son-in-law of a zamindar, is a poet and music-lover. With a deep regard for folk culture, he learns to play the dholak from the aged village headman, Baiju, and mingles with the village folk—much to the distaste of his wife Leela Devi. Shivnath tolerates the mounting tension at home for the sake of his young daughter Neena. But matters come to a head when Leela Devi lets loose a reign of terror, burning down the village. Shivnath walks out of the house.

The next time he returns to meet his child he finds Baiju's daughter in the clutches of Leela Devi's munim. Shivnath kills the clerk and goes to jail for fourteen years to atone for the crime.

His wife and daughter move to the city. Neena does not know

that her father is in prison; she has been told he has become a sadhu.

One day Shivnath hears his daughter, about to marry the prison doctor, express her longing for her father's blessings at the marriage. He also overhears her express her distrust and fear of criminals.

Released on the eve of Neena's marriage, Shivnath joins a procession of beggars, including Baiju, going to the zamindar's house.

Neena distributes coins to them. One after the other, the outstretched hands receive the coins and withdraw—only one hand rises to bless the young bride.

After that Shivnath collapses. Baiju reveals his identity. Neena wishes to take him home but Shivnath prefers to lie under the open sky, serenity on his face as death approaches him.

'I will do it, Hrishi,' Ashok Kumar said as soon as Hrishikesh stopped.

And Ashok Kumar became Shivnath. He lived the role, underplaying the melodramatic edges of the character and controlling situations. Of course, the director too was alert, and *Aashirwad* turned out to be a memorable affair. And the promise asserted by Hrishikesh at the very beginning came true: Ashok Kumar indeed got the Bharat Award for the Best Actor from the president of India.

One is lost in admiration for the veteran who became a child among children as he sang the whimsical, heartwarming song penned by Harindranath Chattopadhyay:

Rail gaadi
Rail gaadi
Rail gaadi chhuk chhuk chhuk chhuk
Beech wale
Station bole
Ruk ruk ruk ruk Ruk ruk ruk ruk...

So far Ashok Kumar's innumerable fans were young men and ladies, men and women. With *Aashirwad* his fans increased and soon Ashok started saying, 'Look look, my fans are growing younger! The majority of them now belong to the age group of six to eight!'

Under the direction of Hrishikesh Mukherjee, the dimension of Ashok Kumar's genius widened as he went from one demanding role to another, in *Satyakam* (1969), *Mili* (1975), *Arjun Pandit* (1976) and *Khubsoorat* with a beautiful Rekha for his co-star.

It is then natural that Ashok Kumar is fond of Hrishikesh Mukherjee who, in his turn, has the highest respect for the artiste in Dadamoni.

Ashok did many many more films but the rest do not fall under the category of excellence. A list of all the films he has been in is appended at the end of this book.

Now that the small screen rules the world of entertainment, Ashok Kumar could not stay out of its mini frame. But he has been very very selective.

So far he has acted in two major serials—*Bahadur Shah Zafar* directed by B.R. Chopra and his son Ravi Chopra; and *Bhim Bhavani* directed by Basu Chatterjee. The third serial that he was associated with—*Hum Log*—was one of the first indigenous soap operas. It attained a special degree of acceptance and artistry because of Ashok Kumar's commentary and summing up at the beginning and end of each episode.

The legendary actor has not stopped yet. Ashok Kumar continues to put on make-up, stand before the camera and charge the screen with his performance...

After floating down the river, he has now reached the ocean...

CHAPTER 12

A MAN OF MANY ROLES

Ashok Kumar has played many roles as an actor. He has played many other roles—as a man. He is an actor because acting is his profession, yes, but he knows many other things and could have been in many other professions, many a vocation.

The Chess Player

Ashok could have been a big name in the world of sports, as a chess player. Once in 1946, or may be 1947, the famed actress Kanan Devi introduced an actor named Iftikhar to Ashok, in Calcutta. Iftikhar had played the hero in two or three films there. When Ashok took over Bombay Talkies, Iftikhar came to Bombay to meet him and they had been friends ever since, until Iftikhar's death in 1994.

Iftikhar taught Ashok how to play chess. Initially he was continuously defeated.

One day Ashok disappeared and did not meet Iftikhar for about a week. During that week Ashok bought a book on chess from Thacker's Bookshop, close to his house at Kala Ghoda, and learnt all the moves by heart. A week later he invited Iftikhar and director Vasant Joglekar to a game of chess. Iftikhar took it for granted that Ashok will lose as usual. Imagine his surprise, and that of Joglekar too, when Ashok won four consecutive games!

The Astrologer

Kunjalal, Ashok's father, was well conversant with astrology and palmistry. Ashok learnt astrology from him and for that he had to learn Sanskrit since all the ancient books on Hindu astrology are in Sanskrit.

He could not study palmistry thoroughly for want of time, but he is quite adept in astrology.

Sadat Hasan Manto, a leading light of Urdu literature, wrote about Ashok Kumar in *Meena Bazaar* (1962). He quotes this incident about Ashok's knowledge of astrology:

> One day after studying Manto's chart, Ashok asked him, 'Are you married?'
>
> 'Don't you know?' Manto countered, wondering at the question.
>
> After a while, Ashok again asked, 'Manto, you don't have any child yet?'
>
> Intrigued, Manto urged, 'What's the matter, please tell me frankly?'
>
> 'Look,' Ashok then revealed, 'a person whose stars are in this particular formation will have a boy first but the child will die.'

Manto admitted that Ashok was right, for his first child was a baby boy who died within a year.

Ashok is a firm believer in the power of astrology. He relied on it even while picking horses at the races. But he has never put more than a hundred rupees on the races—and he has never lost a race.

I would like to testify to what the celebrated Manto has written about Dadamoni's picking winning horses. This happened in 1964. I was visiting Dadamoni on the sets of some film being shot in Roopsri Studio at Dadar, to know if he would accept the role of Bikash, the hero in *Bandini*. I was sent by Bimalda as Dadamoni was taking time to say 'yes'.

I met Dadamoni in the make-up room. He asked me to sit

there while talking to his driver. He gave a slip of paper to the man and ordered him to give it to his mother who was then staying with Kishore Kumar at Juhu. I could gather from his words that they were names of some horses on which his mother should bet the next day, a Sunday.

After the driver left I asked Dadamoni, 'Does Mashima go to the races?'

'Yes, she does,' Dadamoni smiled. 'So does Sati (S. Mukherjee's wife) and of course Shobha (Dadamoni's wife), for the excitement and fun of it. But there is a limit to the bet-money even if they have the chance of earning lakhs. They would not turn gamblers.'

'But how could you be so sure about these horses you named to them?' I was curious. 'How do you feel that they would win? By studying their pedigree or their previous records?'

'None of these but by astrology, by numerology,' Dadamoni said.

I was startled. 'How can you be sure, Dadamoni? Tomorrow, on the 14th, so many horses will run. Is it possible to calculate which one will win?'

'Yes, Nabendu,' Dadamoni nodded, 'it is possible, though I am still not completely successful. But it is a fact that the universe, its creation, sustenance and destruction are all controlled mathematically, precisely and meticulously.'

My respect for Dadamoni reached its zenith that day as I got an insight into his serious and probing mind.

Dadamoni laughed and added, 'Note down the names Nabendu, and go to the races tomorrow. Put down ten rupees on these two horses and you will surely win about Rs 350.'

'I have not yet visited a race course, Dadamoni,' I confessed to him.

With a twinkle in his eyes Dadamoni said, 'You are a writer, Nabendu, you must experience what a race course is. Go there tomorrow with a friend, you will earn enough for your taxi fare and dinner in a good hotel.'

I promised to go and noted down the names of the horses. But the next day I could not go because I could not get hold of any friend. Yet, out of curiosity I looked up the newspaper the following morning, and was amazed to find that two of the horses Dadamoni had named, had won. I was convinced by what Dadamoni had asserted—yes, everything in this universe is a matter of mathematics.

The Painter

Once Ashok complained to Iftikhar that he was feeling bored. Iftikhar asked, 'Tell me, what are your hobbies?'

'None,' Ashok replied.

Iftikhar stared at Ashok. 'Dadamoni, why don't you start drawing or painting?'

Ashok shrugged. 'How can I? I know nothing about painting.'

Iftikhar looked around and picked up a copper vessel from a nearby table. 'Look at this katora,' he said, 'and start drawing that.'

That's how casually it started. Soon Ashok developed an interest in painting, and even started liking it. In a sense it was like Gurudev Tagore, who started painting late in years and learnt all by himself. Ashok's paintings had the mark of distinction and merited to be shown in an exhibition. But Ashok is not keen about that. He does not even paint regularly. Only now and then, when he is bored, he picks up the brush and then he is seized by a kind of passion. He has painted a lot of nudes, all from imagination. He has also painted a Mona Lisa but she too is nude!

The paintings wait to be assessed by an art critic.

The Lover of Vintage Cars

Fascination for antique pieces denotes an extraordinary taste and a special personality. In this respect, Ashok Kumar is indeed special.

Besides two modern cars which are always on the move, Ashok has in his garage an old Riley and a Daimler, both of 1940 vintage. They are kept bright and shining and look like two highbrow aristocrats. They refuse to move although they can, for they are privileged with extra love and care by Ashok Kumar.

One day Ashok came across a Rolls Royce. That particular car was called The Silver Phantom—it was a 12-cylinder car, 22 feet long, one had to talk to the driver through a telephone. That car was one of only seven custom-made Rolls Royces. Ashok saw the car at the Gaekwads and when he heard that the Maharani would sell it, he expressed his desire to possess it.

The price of the car was Rs 49,000. The Maharani gave away the car to Ashok for only Rs 25,000 and said, 'I am giving it to you at the price I bought it for.'

The Rolls Royce came to Ashok Kumar.

The car had two engines. Both the engines would become active when started but after it had run awhile one of the engines would stop, only six cylinders would be active and when the first engine became too hot, the second engine had to be started, switching off the first one. In other words, the car would go on and on, non-stop. There was a gadget whereby the car could be raised up to 15 inches without affecting the chassis, and the petrol tank had a capacity of 50 gallons.

When the company stopped the manufacture of that model, it offered to buy back the car from Ashok Kumar, for a sum of Rs 2 crore. Ashok said, 'No.'

The car is now kept in Delhi, with one Mr Bakshi, a friend of Ashok, and whenever he goes to Delhi, he enjoys a ride in his Rolls Royce. The car, a 1930 model, is now sixty-five years old!

The Linguist

Ashok Kumar was an admirer of Ronald Coleman and Sir Charles Laughton. On his first trip to London, he made a courtesy call to Laughton. He was not a 'Sir' then. Ashok was staying at India House and would invite the British actor for lunch or at times for dinner, for Laughton was fond of Indian food. He would respond heartily and come with his wife.

Ashok once asked him 'Tell me, how can I act better since I am a newcomer.'

Laughton laughed as he replied, 'Do I know how to act better? I do as I feel good and I continue to be there because people like what I do. The day they stop liking it, they will throw me out.'

Ashok said, 'Really? And you say the same to newcomers?'

'Yes, I do,' Laughton replied. 'And I also tell them to know their language more than their mothers. One can improvise better if one has complete control over one's language.'

Ashok was deeply impressed by Laughton's words. After returning to India, Ashok got hold of an Urdu teacher since Urdu was dominant in the dialogues being written at that time. He felt convinced that the pronunciation of Urdu words should be perfect. With this end in view, he started to learn Persian too.

Learning languages was like a wonderful high for Ashok Kumar. While working with the German technicians he had learnt German. One day while travelling with Iftikhar, Ashok noticed a French book on the passenger seat of his friend's car.

'What is this doing here?' he demanded of Iftikhar.

'I'm learning French on the linguaphone,' he informed.

Ashok also started to learn French. He named the youngest of his three daughters 'Pale Etoile' (Pale Star) which later turned into 'Palu', the pet name of Priti who took to essaying comic roles after graduating from the Film and Television Institute of India in Pune.

He had earlier learnt Sanskrit in order to study astrology. And of course he knows Bengali, English and Hindi. That means, in all, Ashok speaks eight languages.

The Homeopath

Yes, Ashok practises homeopathy for himself and friends. He has passed an examination too.

Around 1960–61, the renowned surgeon Dr Shantilal Shah told a pretty fourteen-year-old girl that her leg would have to be amputed. 'Now, who will marry her after that!' her father lamented to Ashok.

Ashok said, 'I have never treated gangrene but let me try.' Under his medication the leg, which had turned black, returned to normalcy, in six months' time.

The doctor asked the girl, 'Who cured you?'

She said, 'Ashok Kumar.'

'The actor?' was his incredulous response.

There are many such cases.

The Singer

Music was in his blood. His maternal grandfather and his mother were great singers. In fact his grandfather had got an Ustad from Banaras to train his two daughters Luna (pet name of Gauri Rani) and Bina (mother of Arun Mukherjee) in music. Ashok also could sing pretty well. If he had concentrated on singing, like Kishore, perhaps he too would have become an immortal singer.

His most famous song is *'Mera bulbul so raha hai...'* in *Kismet*.

The Limericist

Ashok Kumar is a very affable person. He had wonderful communication with his children as well as his brothers and sisters. He used to compose nonsensical rhymes and recite them with either his son Aroop, or Palu, his youngest daughter, in the form of question and answer. Here's one he used to recite with Aroop in Hindi:

Ashok:	*Tumhara naam kya hai beta?*
	(What's your good name my son?)
Aroop:	*Alamtola Baba.*
	(It is Alamtola, O father)
Ashok:	*Tum khata kya hai beta?*
	(What is it that you eat my son?)
Aroop:	*Ghee ka gola Baba.*
	(Balls of clarified butter, dear father)
Ashok:	*Tum sota kahan hai beta?*
	(Where do you sleep my son?)
Aroop:	*Lal palang par Baba.*
	(On the red bedstead, father)
Ashok:	*Tumhari aurat kahan hai beta?*
	(And where be your wife, son?)
Aroop:	*Maa ke ghar mein Baba.*
	(At her mother's, dear father)
Ashok:	*To lata kyon nahin beta?*
	(Why don't you bring her home, O son?)
Aroop:	*U bhag-bhag jaati Baba.*
	(She keeps running away, O father)
Ashok:	*To maarta kyon nahin beta?*
	(Why don't you beat her, my son?)
Aroop:	*Dil ki pyari hai Baba.*
	(She has a wonderful heart, O Baba)

Besides Palu, Ashok Kumar used to call Priti by many names, all in Bengali. Here's a list: Bablukuchu (Little Bablu), Hoonbatashi (Whirlwind), Abol Tabol (Meaningless), Dantabikash (Evergrinning), Mantarini (One who elevates the mind), Jagyapishi (very capable paternal aunt), Domdibili (??), RuiKatla (Rohu-Catla), Boibandil (Bundle of Books), Hankur Pankur (The Fidgeting One). And here's a Bengali rhyme composed with Palu:

Ashok:	*Achha Palumaa, Bablukuchur naamti ki-re?*
	(Palumaa, what is the name of Bablukuchu?)
Palu:	*Bablukuchui naamtire.*
	(It's Bablukuchu, Baba)
Ashok:	*Bablukuchur aar naam kire?*
	(What's the other name of Bablukuchu?)
Palu:	*Naam dhaam kichhu janina re.*
	(I know not any other name or address)
Ashok:	*Bablukuchu ki khaye re?*
	(What it is that Bablukuchu eats?)
Palu:	*Alubhaja diye ghee-bhat re.*
	(Fried potatoes with ghee and rice)
Ashok:	*Bablukuchu aar ki khaye re?*
	(What else does Bablukuchu have?)
Palu:	*Kakhono sakhono maar-taar re.*
	(A beating, now and then)
Ashok:	*Bablukuchu jaaye kothay re?*
	(Where does Bablukuchu go?)
Palu:	*Palki kore bajhye re.*
	(To the loo, seated in a palanquin)
Ashok:	*Bablukuchu aar kothay jaaye re?*
	(Where else does Bablukuchu go?)
Palu:	*Phuler ghaye murchha jaaye re.*
	(Into a swoon when struck by a flower)
Ashok:	*Bablukuchu ki bhabey re?*
	(What does Bablukuchu ponder on?)
Palu:	*Akash-pataal-martya re.*
	(The sky, the earth, the nether world)
Ashok:	*Bablukuchur baap ke re?*
	(Pray who is the father of Bablukuchu?)
Palu:	*Nrisimhavatar shey re.*
	(None but the incarnation of Narisimha)
Ashok:	*Bablukuchur maa key re?*
	(And who'd be Bablukuchu's mother?)

Palu: *Kalir Taraka, Baap re!*
(She is a modern version of demoness Taraka, O Dad)

Ashok used to have such rhyme-duets with each of his children and with his brothers too. Ashok does not recall the others but here's one he used to recite with Anoop—a word rhythmically uttered by the two of them, in quick succession, mounting higher and higher in a crescendo:

Ashok: Tan
Anoop: Abol
Ashok: Abol
Anoop: Raat
Ashok: Morabba
Anoop: Din
Ashok: Achar
Anoop: Seem
Ashok: Maseek
Anoop: Juloon
Ashok: Magreeb
Anoop: Kaan
Ashok: Taroo
Anoop: Bandar
Ashok: Maam
Anoop: Kabaddar
Ashok: Dupahar
Anoop: Chatni
Ashok: Qutub
Anoop: Min-a-a-r

That's what Ashok Kumar is—a man who wants to be happy and make others happy. One who believes: 'If you are happy, be happy even for five minutes.'

CHAPTER 13

AN ACTOR'S ROLE IN CINEMA

Know thyself. The words are scribbled on the walls of the ancient temple of Apollo in Delphi. Long before that, the Hindus said 'Atmaanam Viddhi'. Meaning, once again, 'Know thyself'.

A man reads fiction, listens to ballads, watches a play on the stage—all, to know about himself. He learns by reading, by hearing and by seeing. The last in particular because knowledge is best grasped by seeing: we learn best when we see something with our own eyes. And the best mode of seeing is cinema, for it is the synthesis of all art forms: its principal components are literature, painting, drama and music. Cinema combines the artistry of many, perhaps that is why it is the most intoxicating of artistic experiences or Rasas.

But why does man want to know himself? Because man does not know himself completely. By reading, by hearing and by watching himself he learns about the ever-increasing, ever-changing complexities of life. Its realities are changing all around him, yet in its elements life remains the same.

Man loves all beautiful things on earth but most of all he loves himself. Every man is a Narcissus. Thus every man wants to learn about himself, about his inner desires and obsessions, about his good deeds as well as sins, about his ideals and crimes, about what to do and what not to, by watching man in action before his eyes.

He learns about himself through sensations pleasing and painful. That is why cinema is the most popular medium in this century, extending its vista through video and television.

But life in cinema is enacted by actors and actresses. They impersonate characters, they generate different emotions in the viewers by their performance. And that is why they become popular and win the love and respect of people.

A film-actor, like the stage-actor, lays stress on two things, according to Bharat Muni, the author of *Natya Shastra*: Angika, the body movements, and Vachika or dialogue delivery. Through these two equipments he attempts to reveal the mind and soul of the dramatis persona. The most exacting of artistes at times identifies so completely with the character that he or she thinks he *is* the character. At the same time he adds to the character the extra dimension of his own individuality. This distinct stamp of individuality determines the actor or actress's 'acting style'.

Ashok's Acting Style

Ashok Kumar has a distinct acting style which is absolutely natural, life-like. 'I dislike being melodramatic,' he asserts. 'I prefer the quiet style.'

Ashok Kumar's actions and dialogue delivery are always measured. 'I have never believed in theories, never felt the need for a definition. I never sat down to think of the acting process.'

Ashok takes the scene, rehearses the lines, plans the body movement and repeats them on the set the next day. This has been his effort since the Bombay Talkies days.

In *Gumraah*, director B.R. Chopra narrated a scene that required him to sit between his wife, being played by Mala Sinha, and her lover, Sunil Dutt. They would be silent while Ashok would go on talking incessantly, telling his wife to hurry up with the tea and so on. For the next three days Ashok improvised the scene at home, driving his wife Shobha crazy. He kept on telling her to hurry up with the tea until she was ready to hit him with the kettle. He jotted down the lines as he had said to B.R. Chopra. When Shobha saw the film, she said, 'Why do you have to make our private life public?'

'My effort,' Ashok sums up, 'has always been to act naturally. I behave onscreen the way I would at home.' Ashok never tires of learning. In the early years Devika Rani once told him, 'You shake your head too much. That disturbs the viewer watching you on screen. Move your head but slowly.' Ashok pondered over her words, watched himself on the moviola, absorbed the truth of Devika Rani's words and showed his appreciation by shaking his head less, and slower.

In this manner he learnt many a thing from stalwarts like Debaki Bose, Sushil Mazumdar who was himself a first-rate actor, and Amar Mallik of New Theatres who guided his pronunciation of Bengali dialogue. He keeps his eyes and ears ever open, observing the men around him, noting their reactions on the sets and learning from that. Once, while he was delivering a dialogue, a lightman laughed out aloud. It spoilt the shot. Peeved, Ashok walked up to the man and asked him, 'What made you laugh? I did not mean to be funny!' The man said, 'Dadamoni, you were looking very odd.' Ashok went to the greenroom, watched himself speak the line while repeating the action in the 'Take'. The lightman was not wrong, he admitted to himself. When he corrected himself and gave the take, the lightman grinned and saluted him.

Ashok always insists on being informed beforehand, he must prepare for a scene. Much like a baby, who is very accommodating but must be fed at the right time. He cannot work in chaotic circumstances. 'That's something I have not got used to,' he says, 'despite all these years. I guess I am still learning. Every role can be done in so many different ways. One has to discover the way the audience will like it best.' On the other hand, he says, 'I am never conscious that we are all players, performing before a public.

Instead I play from the heart, I talk-walk-think before the camera as I would beyond its range.'

A consummate actor makes the viewers feel the mind and soul of the character he portrays. He makes them share the anguish, the joy, the sorrow, the elation and frustration of the character intensely. Ashok Kumar does that, and to such an extent that he can be classed among the all-time greats in film-acting.

Some Awards

Ashok Kumar laughs as he says, 'Such strange things happen in life! The man who was unhappy with his acting ability for years, one day got the Best Actor's award! It sounds unbelievable. Imagine someone assuring me in 1935–36 that I would earn awards for good acting, even the Best Actor's—would I have believed him? But I did get it one day! Life, at moments, turns into a strange fiction.'

His first award came from the Sangeet Natak Akademi. Then came the Padmashri in 1962, the year of Indo-Chinese confrontation. Babu Rajendra Prasad, the then president of India, had put the Gold Medal around the actor's neck.

Earlier Ashok had received a letter from the ministry seeking his willingness to accept the award. But he did not divulge this to anyone. When the names of those honoured with Padmashri came out in the papers, an ecstatic Kunjalal called up his son: 'Have you seen the newspaper, Ashok? You are going to get a Padmashri!' Kunjalal was so thrilled he would have flown to Ashok if he had wings. He was then in Bombay, staying with Kishore Kumar.

Ashok had already seen the papers.

Kunjalal kept repeating, 'See the papers, Ashok! Read, read your name!'

After receiving the award in Delhi, when Ashok landed in Bombay, he drove straight to his father.

Kunjalal rushed towards his elder son while telling Kishore excitedly, 'Bow down to Ashok, touch his feet Kishore—Ashok is now a Padmashri!'

Ashok had no yearning for any awards, ever. But of course he was happy to receive them.

He got the National award for Best Actor in 1964, for his role in B.R. Chopra's *Gumraah*. And in 1968 he got the award a second time, for his role in *Aashirwad*. But the two awards Ashok is particularly proud of are the prestigious Dada Saheb Phalke Award—the highest honour in Indian cinema—he got in 1989, and the Maratha Gaurav Award bestowed by the Maharashtra Government.

He now says, 'I have no more longing for any award, but I still have the desire to act in a worthwhile role.'

Outstanding Popularity

In 1936, after *Achhut Kanya* Ashok Kumar became the idol for school and college students. College boys would stroll around singing, *'Tu ban ki chidiyan, mai ban ka panchhi, ban ke ban ban bolun re'e'e...'*

The same Ashok Kumar who would fumble in the beginning gradually revealed his talents to emerge as the classic, languorous lover of the Indian screen.

Sadat Hasan Manto writes in his *Meena Bazaar* about an unusual admirer:

> A certain bold lady took Ashok Kumar home hoping to win him over. But he was so very firm that she had to change her tactics. She told him, instead, 'I was just testing you, you see! You are my brother!'

Ashok Kumar was never a flirt. He just did not have the guts to be one! Which was very surprising, considering that hundreds of young women adored him. He used to get love-letters from thousands. But, to the best of my knowledge, he has not read more than a hundred out of this heap!

Ashok Kumar's popularity grew by the day. Because he seldom appeared in public, because he mostly kept to himself, when people did get a glimpse of him, they were riotous. The traffic would come to a halt because the crowd of admirers refused to budge. There were even occasions when the police had to resort to lathi-charge.

Manto has also written about the post-Partition incident, recounted earlier in this book, when the two were caught in a procession late one night, in a Muslim area. Ashok had then expressed his faith in the viewers, saying, 'You got frightened unnecessarily—people don't question artistes.' I was therefore surprised by an incident I was witness to, sometime in the June of 1951.

I was travelling with Dadamoni from his residence at Kala Ghoda to VT station. We were to take a train to Matheran where we were to discuss the script of *Kafila* along with its director, Aravind Sen. As soon as the pedestrians noticed Ashok Kumar, they started to chant and cry out:

Ashok Kumar!
There goes Ashok Kumar!
Oh Ashok Kumar!
Hello Ashok Kumar!

But to every excited exclamation, Ashok angrily replied:

Shut up!
Damn you!
Go to hell.

Ashok reclined, merging with the seat in order to avoid being seen. I laughed as I asked him, 'Dadamoni, why do you resent the admiration of the public?'

Ashok Kumar replied, 'I am fed up. For so many years now they have been doing this whenever they see me—Ashok Kumar, Ashok Kumar, Ashok Kumar! The call now irritates me.'

I said, 'Dadamoni, I'm sure an intelligent person like you knows why they do so?'

Ashok said, 'I know, but they invade my privacy. I am not an actor all the time.'

'You are arguing like a child, sir,' I reasoned again. 'For the viewers, you are always Ashok Kumar the actor. They have a personal image of you formed from the roles you have enacted on screen. More importantly, they are deeply impressed by you, by your performances. They love you. You are more popular with them than even a political leader. Their cries are love-calls. You are a fortunate man, their calls are God's whispers.'

Ashok frowned, 'Have you seen God?'

'Oh no,' I said, 'but I feel he exists.'

Ashok said, emphasising his words, 'I have not yet met him nor do I feel him!'

'I withdraw my reference to God,' I immediately responded, 'but the rest of my dialogue remains intact. Please, I request you, apply your extraordinary reasoning power and desist from your angry reactions to the public. It is they you owe your success to.'

With a smile Ashok Kumar looked at Aravind Sen, the director, and said, 'Nabendu argues well. After all, he is a good writer. All right, Nabendu, I will consider your arguments.'

There ended our talks for the moment. But after that I never saw Dadamoni react angrily, nor heard anyone speak of such a reaction.

An Admirer of Other's Talent

Ashok Kumar has a rare quality: he has always admired talent in others. This came to the fore when he, as a producer, offered a platform to so many directors and artistes.

As an actor he has always paid compliments to Dilip Kumar, Raj Kapoor, Dev Anand. About the 'current' actors, he says, 'There is no doubt that Amitabh Bachchan is a great actor. I liked him in *Mili* and some of his angry young man roles... Anil Kapoor is fine... Among the girls I have liked Rekha, now I like Madhuri Dixit. She is lovely, she has a subdued screen presence...'

What Film Personalities Say About Him

B.R. Chopra: Film-maker

His greatest quality is that he puts in a lot of effort to get the effect of effortless acting. I consider him a pioneer of the natural style of acting—whatever he did or spoke came very naturally, right from his first film, *Jeevan Naiya*. Perhaps the fact that he did not want to act, and his training under foreign directors, helped him develop this skill.

Hrishikesh Mukherjee: Director-Editor

His sincerity always touches me. You know, he is allergic to spirit gum. He can't wear a beard or moustache for any length of time. But while shooting for *Aashirwad*, he did not once complain although he had to keep the beard on day after day, shot after shot, under the hot sun.

He can be temperamental too. When I started shooting *Aashirwad*, he came to the sets late on the first two days. I warned him that I would not take it. But he was late again. On the fourth day when I yelled at him, he put on a sad face and said he had been coming late because of a quarrel with his wife. I believed him of course. But you know what an actor Ashok Kumar is! When I called up his wife to inquire what the matter was, she said she had not met him for the last four days!

I had caught Dadamoni redhanded. But charming as he is, he

replied blushing, 'Now that you have caught me out, please don't blow it up.' After that he was never late.

He is young in mind and at heart—and that is what makes him Ashok Kumar. His role in *Khubsoorat* is based on his own character! A man outwardly serious but inwardly very humorous. He is the oldest and the youngest at the same time.

Shakti Samanta: Producer-Director

Even in my college days Dadamoni was my favourite actor. I saw all his Bombay Talkies films—*Jhoola, Bandhan, Kangan* and *Kismet*, which I must have seen at least seven times at Calcutta's Roxy cinema. Since then I have been a fan of Dadamoni. I dreamt of joining Bombay Talkies. Fortunately, when I did, he had already taken over as one of the directors. It was a big moment for me when Phani Mazumdar, with whom I was working, introduced me to Dadamoni.

Later, when I became a director, I realised what an absolute professional he is. He refuses to shoot if the dialogues are not given a day in advance, for he likes to work out the delivery beforehand. When I was making the bilingual *Anand Ashram* (in Hindi and Bengali), Dadamoni said to Uttam Kumar, 'Look, Uttam, you are supposed to be the finest actor in Bengal, and I don't know any Bengali. This man has "phasaoed" (trapped) me into a double version. You must help me with the dialogue so that I don't look a novice.' Uttam answered, 'Dadamoni, why are you pulling my leg? Haven't I already seen your work in Tapanda's *Haatey Bajarey*?'

Ashok Kumar believes in teamwork. He is extremely cooperative with his co-artistes, even newcomers. He will rehearse a scene as many times as a co-artiste wants to. But there is one little problem: he cannot work after 6.30 p.m. And this can be a major problem these days when an artiste often reports at 6 p.m. for a 9 a.m. shift! But Dadamoni says, 'What can I do? This is my time to go to the bathroom—(that's where he does all his thinking and creative work too). So what can I do?'

Basu Chatterjee: An Avant-garde Director Who Is Commercially Successful

It is fun working with Ashok Kumar. Always cooperative on the sets, he sometimes jokes with us, 'Why do you take me? I am so old, I cannot remember my lines...' Actually, he has no problem whatsoever!

He has several interests other than films. Music, painting, astrology... He still goes to parties, whereas I don't feel like it anymore!

There are many factors to explain why he has survived so long. He always keeps himself upto date on his times, on what is going on around him. He is ready to adapt, and has worked on television unlike many. Small wonder, he has worked with three generations of film-makers!

Pran: One of the Finest Character Actors of the Indian Screen

My first film with Ashok Kumar was *Afsana*. He was a young man then. From then to now, I find no difference in him. He had childlike ways then, he has childlike ways now. When the director hands him his dialogue, he will say, 'What is this? I can't speak these lines...' Then he speaks those very lines and exactly the way the director wants him to! But not before teasing him.

From the vey beginning he has shown his affection for me. As for me, it is difficult to express in words how fond I am of him. I don't have the same feelings for any other artiste. When we were doing *Victoria No. 203*, there was not just friendship between the two characters we played but telepathy! One would start a dialogue and the other would pick it up. The improvisation and teamwork were so good, it was simply fun! I don't think there has been a crime-comedy like this film before—nor will there be one again.

Those days there was a family-like atmosphere at work. We would meet, talk, spend time together... Unlike today. These days we leave home at 7 and return at 2 a.m, working three shifts a day! It is all very different...

His Studio-cum-Study

Books, newspapers, magazines, scripts, scenes with dialogues for the next day's shoot, canvases and painting materials. Everything is there, waiting for Ashok Kumar. When he returns home in the evening, or when there is no shooting, he locks himself in, seats himself on the pot in the middle of the room, and proceeds to read or paint, prepare for the next day or indulge in creative thinking.

Yes, it is his bathroom but only due to the presence of the potty and the shower-bath. For all practical purposes, it is his studio-cum-study! 'This is where the star churns out his creations!' he says to his intimate friends, pointing with a grin on his face to his 'throne'—the potty.

A Man of 'Business'

Apart from film production, Ashok Kumar tried his hand at business too, for many people look down upon 'films' as 'gambling' rather than 'business'.

He was involved in the manufacture of shaving blades and cigarettes. He has been an agent of foreign musical instruments. And once, he was the owner of the largest chicken firm in Asia!

But all these businesses were like games to him. He gave up all of them. For, intrinsically Ashok Kumar is not a businessman but an artist.

Miles to Walk...? Not for Him

'One hobby I don't have is walking!' Ashok Kumar once said. He narrated an incident that made him decide against it.

'We had gone to Kashmir to picturise *Kalpana* (my own production which featured both Padmini and Ragini). There we were invited to dinner by a boatman named Koro. His father was 100 years old. His wife—his second marriage—was eighty-five years old. My friend Iftekhar drew a portrait of his wife and presented it to him.

'That was in 1959. Ten years later, when we went there with Sadhana for the shooting of *Inteqam*, I met Koro's father once again. By then his second wife was also dead. I asked him if he had any intention of marrying again, since he seemed to be still going strong. He said, "I eat well and save all my energy by sitting in one place." That's when I decided: in order to save my energy—I should not do any walking!'

Something Foul

His daughter Priti Ganguly reveals a little known aspect of Ashok Kumar's personality.

'He has a foul temper though he rarely loses it,' she says. 'But when he does, we are left with smashed pieces of all our best China.'

Once, however, this resulted in a truly amusing incident. This was after the veteran had just had a petty quarrel with his wife, Shobha. Ashok was about to fling a prize crystal vase against the wall when Priti intervened. 'Don't, Baba!' she pleaded, 'It's real crystal!' Ashok stopped in his track, stared at the vase and told Priti, 'Give me a cheap one.'

Priti dutifully did so, and Ashok Kumar's 'foul' temper crashed into pieces against the wall!

CHAPTER 14

HIS MANY MANY HEROINES

Devika Rani, Maya Devi, Leela Chitnis, Renuka Devi, Mumtaz Shanti, Veena, Naseem, Nargis, Rehana, Suraiya, Kanan Devi, Madhubala, Sumitra Devi, Nalini Jaywant, Geeta Bali, Kamini Kaushal, Meena Kumari, Bina Rai, Bhanumati, Nirupa Roy, Nutan, Padmini, Shyama, Mala Sinha, Suchitra Sen, Vyjayantimala: the list of his leading ladies is by no means short.

He has at least a pack of films with each of the memorable names above. With Nirupa Roy, he did no less than fifteen films. And Meena Kumari was his heroine in eighteen films.

Ashok has showered compliments, now and again, on Leela Chitnis, Meena Kumari and Suchitra Sen. Yet, he says, he had no favourite among his leading ladies, 'because my performance has never been affected by my co-stars. To me, acting was just a job, which I did to the best of my ability.' But he did share a professional rapport with Meena Kumari—'She was a quick learner and an intelligent artist,' he adds.

Nirupa Roy and Meena Kumari both said they had mastered the art of acting from Ashok Kumar. 'I was terribly nervous when I was paired with Ashok Kumar for the first time (in *Bhai Bhai*, made in 1950),' says Nirupa Roy. 'He was a superstar and I a mere beginner. But he was so reassuring that I was soon at ease. I learnt a lot from him. Dialogue delivery, for one. But in all the fifteen films we have done together, we have played the stock role of husband and wife!'

Regarding Meena Kumari, Ashok Kumar says, 'In the early days she used to overact, there was a touch of theatricality. I pointed it out to her while we were doing *Tamasha*. She said, "Tell me then, how to do it." So I started to teach her. She was an eager learner. And she learnt so well that she rose to be one of the greatest. And then she had that wonderful voice. It was so sweet!'

When it comes to acting, Ashok Kumar places Meena Kumari after Geeta Bali and Madhubala—both of them he considers as Numero Uno. He has compliments for Suchitra Sen and Nutan too.

Affairs of the Heart?

The number of film magazines in Indian languages is countless. One cannot even recall all the names. But most of these magazines have one trait in common: they all thrive on scandals relating to the lives of actors and actresses. This is so to such an extent that people believe some actors and actresses ensure that their names appear in print now and then, through such scandals.

And if people relish scandal to such an extent, one might want to know whether Ashok Kumar was ever involved in a scandal—whether real, fabricated or manipulated?

Once in the 1950s Baburao Patel, editor and publisher of India's first film trade magazine *Filmindia* (1935–61), took to Ashok Kumar bashing. The magazine wrote things about him when he was away in Cairo with Nalini Jaywant to shoot for *Naaz*. But the other papers never reported any affairs of the heart involving Ashok.

This writer was once a party to a piquant situation. It was sometime in 1951. The shooting was over for the day, and I was to accompany Dadamoni to his residence at Kala Ghoda. Dadamoni was driving himself, and the leading lady (one of the top stars of the time) sought a lift, instructing her driver to follow with her car. As soon as this was decided Dadamoni whispered to me, 'Nabendu, go and sit in the front seat—I don't want her to sit by my side.' I had no choice but to obey. And when the heroine saw me in the car she changed her mind. 'Dadamoni, I remember now, I must go my tailor. Sorry,' she said as she sat in her own car and drove away. Dadamoni grinned and said, 'Thanks, Nabendu.'

Ashok Kumar says, 'Actors and actresses have to work in close physical proximity. So such relationships can take place at times.'

But he seems to be immune to this phenomenon. How come?

'The day *Jeevan Naiya* was released, Himanshu Rai made me promise two things,' Ashok explains. 'He said, "Look Ashok, you have become a hero now. And the flappers will start chasing you."'

Ashok was quite innocent in those days. 'Flappers?' he asked, 'What are they, sir?'

Rai gravely said, 'Nubile sixteen-year-olds. Girls will be after you, Ashok.'

'But why, sir?' the young hero asked again.

Rai said, 'That's how it happens—it is a law of nature—these flappers always chase a new "hero". So beware and give me your word that you shall not turn towards them. Always return home by six in the evening and once in, stay in. Keep your hearth burning.'

As he said this, Rai took Ashok's hand in his own, and the young hero gave him his word. Ever since he has returned home in the evening and kept the hearth at his home burning. His wife corroborated this when she said, 'He has always been a homebird. And his strong sense of duty towards his family extended to his brothers, Kishore and Anoop, whom he supported until they established themselves. He still helps relatives with money whenever they need it…'

CHAPTER 15

EVERY JACK HAS HIS JILL

One day while discussing astrology with some friends, Ashok Kumar had said, 'Time determines the horoscope of a person. Had I been born five minutes earlier, I could have been a Maharaja.'

One amongst the friends asked, 'Then why were you born at a different time?'

'Because of my destiny,' Ashok replied.

The man again asked, 'What about marriages, Dadamoni?'

'Don't you know that marriages are made in heaven?' Ashok said with a smile. 'My friend, your destiny again determines who is to be your enemy, your friend and even your wife.'

Ashok Kumar did not know until his marriage who would be his wife but he had met her once when he was an eighteen-year-old student of Law.

Ashok had gone to Bhagalpur where his mother's brothers lived. His eldest Mama Shyam one day visited a friend, one Captain Banerjee, an armyman. Ashok went along with him.

Seated in the living room, Ashok could see a thin, barebodied, pajama-clad girl of about eight deftly rolling rotis in the kitchen. Within the short while that Ashok watched, she had rolled some fifty rotis.

Shyam Mama had whispered back then, 'In middle-class homes even small girls must labour thus.'

Ashok was not pleased to hear that even though he had no inkling that the eight-year-old would grow up to be his dear wife!

In 1934, as soon as Ashok joined Bombay Talkies, his parents started their efforts to get him married. One Patol Babu's daughter in Bhagalpur was found suitable but the negotiations came a cropper when Ashok was cast as the hero of *Jeevan Naiya*. Gouri Rani was then desperate to find a bride for her son. She journeyed to different cities—Jhansi, Agra, Banaras, Patna—in search of a suitable girl. Her eldest brother Shyam had a good friend in Calcutta who was a famous actor. Indu Mukherjee, the friend, had risen to fame by enacting Krishna in the mythological, *Karnarjun*, written by Aparesh Mukherjee. He was also successful as a character actor in Bengali films. He had three daughters—each one pretty as a fairy. Shyam approached Indu Babu: 'We would like to have one of your daughters in our family, Indu.'

Indu said, 'Take whoever you like. But tell me, who is the boy?'

'For our Ashok,' Mama replied.

Indu Mukherjee stared at his friend for a couple of seconds, then turned away his face. 'Forgive me, friend,' he said, 'I shall not give any of my daughters to a film-man. I know what happens in films.'

Ashok heard this and wrote to his mother: 'Don't fix my marriage before I earn Rs 500 to 700 per month.' His parents, of course, paid no heed to this.

One day in April 1938, Ashok received a telegram in Bombay: 'Come immediately to Khandwa. Very urgent. Kunjalal.'

Ashok was then shooting for *Vachan*. But he immediately took leave and set out for Khandwa the same night, worried to death by the unexplained 'urgency' of the telegram.

When the train reached Khandwa, Kunjalal was waiting for him. 'You need not get down,' he said, stepping into the compartment. 'I am also going with you.'

'But where to, father?' Ashok wondered.

Kunjalal chose to say in Hindi, 'Together we shall go to Calcutta.'

Always scared, in his early years, of his father, Ashok dared not ask why they must travel to Calcutta. He resigned himself to his father's hand.

At Jabalpur, Kunjalal seemed to be in a better mood. Speaking once again in Hindi, he said, 'Go and look up your bhabhi in the ladies compartment. See if she requires any help.'

Ashok alighted and met his bhabhi, the wife of a cousin. The son of Kunjalal's sister, his cousin too was a lawyer practising at Khandwa.

Ashok asked her, 'What's up, bhabhi? Why are you all rushing to Calcutta? On what mission?'

Bhabhi could not check her laughter. 'Don't fake ignorance, Ashok!'

'I swear, bhabhi,' Ashok said, 'I don't know anything!'

'What a shame!' Bhabhi laughed heartily. 'My poor devarji, your marriage has been fixed.'

'What!' Ashok laughed aloud at the shock, 'Don't pull my legs.'

'But it is God's truth,' she asserted.

The train whistled its intent to move ahead.

Ashok ran back to his compartment but did not look at his father who sat with a grave face, looking out of the window.

All Gouri Rani said when she saw Ashok in Calcutta was: 'So you have come!'

'What do you mean?' Ashok said in a vexed tone. 'You all have arranged my marriage, wired me to come and I have arrived.'

Gouri Rani watched her son as she queried, 'You will marry, won't you? Or do you want to remain a Devdas?'

Ashok felt irked. 'Why cross-examine me, Maa, you have fixed up the marriage and, I presume, also sent out the invitations?'

'Yes,' said his mother. 'So have the bride's party.'

'And now you are trying to know my mind?' Ashok was offended, it was clear from his tone.

'No, no,' Gouri Rani said, 'see the girl, my son. I wonder if you will like her.'

Ashok shook his head, 'It is meaningless to see the girl now. You have already selected her.'

'No, no, you must see the girl,' Gouri Rani said, stressing every word she spoke, 'or else I will stop this marriage.' She called up her brother, 'Shyam, Ashok will not marry her. Find him a fairer girl.'

'Have you gone crazy, Maa?' Ashok found himself getting angry. 'We are into Wednesday, and the marriage is supposed to be on Friday. And now you are saying that unless I like this girl the marriage will not be ceremonised!'

'Yes, indeed,' Gouri Rani interrupted. 'You must see the girl, and that's the last word.'

Ashok had no choice but to obey.

The girl's family had then put up at a place in Calcutta's Panditia Road. His mother took him there along with Shyam Mama and bhabhi.

Gouri Rani went straight inside the house to see if the girl was all done up to meet her son. Ashok sat in the drawing room along with the others. He suddenly felt shy and started sweating. After quite a while Gouri Rani, assisted by two ladies of the family, ushered the girl into the room. A swift glance revealed to Ashok that the girl was dressed in a purple-coloured silk sari, a Kanan Bala blouse (the design was named after the ageless actress) and a liberal dash of lipstick.

Ashok wanted to take a critical look but could not bring himself to do that, overcome as he was by shyness. When he again looked at the girl, she too was glancing his way. For a moment their eyes locked; the next moment both of them turned away their gaze.

'What is this, Ashok,' Shyam Mama addressed his nephew, 'look at her properly. You know the girl.'

Ashok was startled, 'Oh no, I don't.'

'Oh yes, you know her,' Mama stressed his words. 'Don't you remember that you once visited the house of my friend Captain Banerjee in Bhagalpur? She is the same girl who was rolling rotis.'

Goodness gracious! But she was a girl of eight then, bare-bodied! Oh God, she is eighteen now and Ashok is twenty-eight!

'Don't be shy, Ashok, talk to her,' Shyam Mama said.

'You talk, Mama,' Ashok muttered, 'on my behalf.'

Mama asked the girl: 'Tell Ashok your name, my daughter.'

The girl murmured with a smile, 'Shobha Rani Bandopadhyay.'

'Are you adept at cooking, Shobha?'

Shobha looked up for a second, then replied: 'Oh yes, I can cook both kinds—Bengali as well as English.'

'Wonderful,' Mama responded. 'Now tell me Shobha, can you sing?'

Shobha remained silent.

'Do you?' Mama repeated.

'Yes sir,' Shobha said.

Someone shouted, 'Bring in the harmonium.'

Shobha sang. In those years every girl belonging to the middle class had to learn two or three songs, for it was customary for the elders in the groom's party to ask the girl to sing. If they didn't, the bride's party would urge them to, saying: 'Our girl sings beautifully—people say she puts the cuckoo to shame.'

So the cuckoo named Shobha Rani had to sing. She sang a hit song of her times, sung by Kanan Devi and written by Tagore—*'Aaj sabar range rang meshate habey'* (It is time to blend in your hues with that of the others).

The singer in Ashok Kumar felt that Shobha Rani was not quite in tune, that she had learnt the song, learnt to play the harmonium too, but her heart was not in it. Yet Ashok could not belittle her abilities. He remembered how deftly the girl had rolled the rotis ten years ago! The same girl, now a woman of eighteen. Looks sensitive, yes. Has a kind of charm too. But her singing...

Shobha Rani stopped her song.

Gouri Rani knew that the girl's performance was not upto the mark, so she voiced an excuse. 'I do not appreciate this custom of "Sing a song, daughter". The custom is no longer given any importance in respectable families. But what does Ashok say now, Shyam? His verdict?'

'Yes Ashok, we have liked Shobha,' Mama looked at him. 'Now what is your "verdict", as your mother puts it?'

Ashok glanced once more at Shobha. Shobha too stole a glance at him. Then Ashok stared at the ceiling and muttered, 'I don't dislike her—'

Shobha shyly lowered her face, a smile creeping on to her lips. Others laughed out aloud.

Gouri Rani said, 'Call the Purohit.'

The pandit who would conduct the marriage ceremony came up to draw out the details. 'On which day of the week was Sriman born?' asked the aged pandit.

'Friday,' Gouri Rani informed him.

'Impossible,' the pandit vigorously shook his head. 'There is no question of the marriage being solemnised on the day the groom was born. And there is no second auspicious day within the next two months.'

'But he must get married this time,' Gouri Rani said.

'I can't wait for two months,' Ashok protested. 'I shall leave tomorrow and complete the shooting for *Vachan*.'

Gouri Rani looked sternly at the pandit. 'Please solve the problem, sir,' she said.

The pandit frowned as he looked from one face to another. Then he said, 'In that case, let the marriage be solemnised tomorrow. It is Thursday, and there is an auspicious lagna (hour) for marriage too.'

'But—' Gouri Rani said and stopped.

'But—' Mama also could not complete.

For, Shobha's father was yet to arrive. Sashadhar Mukherjee and Sati Rani were to arrive on Friday! And so many invitees have to be informed!

But there was no other alternative. Gouri Rani would not trust her son to wait for long. He was in films, wasn't he—a hero!

The next day there were no men to run errands, complete the chores or conduct the ceremony. There were only the five persons of the groom's party—Kunjalal, Shyam, bhabhi, her husband and Gouri Rani. Yet, none of these problems came in the way of the auspicious ceremony the next day.

The memorable day was 14 April 1938. The groom's party sat in a room, under a hired old fan that had been installed for the day. It made a horrible screeching noise. In an effort to silence the protestations someone poured some engine oil on the fan.

The pandit had started to chant the mantras. The shehnai party at the gate played with gusto. Perhaps angered by all this, the silent fan now started to throw out the dirty oil along with the cool air. Soon the shirts and kurtas, saris and dhotis, as well as the heads of the invitees in the room were riddled with black spots. They looked like a horde of leopards.

Through all this, the marriage vows were exchanged and the next morning Ashok returned with his destined wife Shobha to their house.

Soon after Sati Rani entered, jubilantly saying, 'So you've agreed to marry, Dadamoni? You are tamed?' Right behind her was Sashadhar. Ashok warmly welcomed them and said, 'Meet my wife Shobha.'

'What! You are supposed to get married today?'

When the story was narrated for their benefit, Sati Rani looked disappointed. She turned to her husband and said, 'Then let us return to Bombay today. What is the point of our coming if the marriage has already taken place?'

Sashadhar laughed, 'So what, we shall attend the Boubhat!' This Boubhat is the function where the bride serves all the senior members of the groom's family, a symbol of her acceptance as a member of the family.

The shehnai played on a happy note.

Shobha personified the graces of Goddess Lakshmi. After their marriage, Ashok's fame went on increasing. So did his remunerations.

Soon they started to come, God's blessings. They came, cried, laughed, wept, and grew up to fill their cups of happiness.

The first child was Bharati. Well educated and happily married, she is the mother of Anuradha Patel who shot into fame for some time as an actress and in 1988, married actor Kanwaljit Singh.

The second one is Aroop. An intelligent man, he learnt about film direction and assisted Basu Chatterjee for some years. At present he runs a business and lives with his wife and children.

Roopa, the third, was the pretty one. She is happily married to producer Deven Verma, who is more celebrated as a comedian in popular films.

The youngest one, Priti—Palu—trained in acting from FTII and shot into limelight. Now married, she conducts an acting school in Bombay.

Shobha was a wonderful woman—a fine specimen of the Sanskrit word for wife: Sahadharmini. She who helps her husband in every righteous act. And what are these righteous acts? The general codes laid down by all religions of the world: to be good and to perform his good job well. Ashok Kumar's job was acting. Shobha attended upon him, saw to it that he leaves home for shooting and when he returned home after the day's work—keeping his promise to the late Himanshu Rai—Shobha welcomed him. She was an image of the Mother Goddess, Annapurna, feeding her lord Shiva. She was a marvellous cook. She loved to cook and talk, cook and serve her love, Ashok Kumar.

Shobha was gracious, intelligent, witty, efficient, ebullient, smiling, radiating charm and inspiring her man and her children. Voices, laughter, music—the home vibrated with their happiness. Worthy elders, worthy brothers, the irreplaceable golden voice of Hindi films and inimitable actor, Kishore Kumar; Anoop Kumar, the other talent in the family; S. Mukherjee, an all-time great producer of India; his wife Sati, their children—it was a union of many families. Every one was successful, respected and loved by society. Above all, there was love for one another. Happiness galore. Life was a honeycomb...

Some time in March 1987, I visited Dadamoni at his Chembur residence. I was commissioned by a Bengali journal to write about him. There I sat in the small kitchen-cum-dining room where Shobha Bhabhi sat near a gas stove and fried fish pakodas for Dadamoni and me. She was quite unwell then and looked it too, yet she kept laughing and talking as if she were absolutely normal.

After we had tea, Dadamoni took me to the covered verandah and said, 'She is very sick Nabendu, her liver, you know...' I nodded.

Dadamoni continued in a monotone, 'I am now giving her homeopathic medicines and she is responding, though slowly. Today is March 18, and the golden jubilee of our marriage will be celebrated in less than a month's time. I hope she enjoys the day.'

Ashok Kumar made a list of the names of a hundred near and dear ones he wanted to be present on 14 April 1987. He printed cards and booked a hundred tables at the Sea Rock Hotel to celebrate the golden day in his life with Shobha.

But Shobha's condition worsened. Doctors who came to attend upon her did not hold out much hope.

Shobha clasped Ashok's hand and said, 'I want to attend our golden-jubilee celebration, please help me, Dadamoni!'

Ashok Kumar tried his best but failed. Shobha breathed her last on 10 April.

Ashok Kumar had no control over his destiny.

Since Shobha's death, Ashok is alone. His son and daughters, they come and go. His friends visit him now and then. His daughter Priti comes and stays with him at times but mostly Ashok Kumar is alone in that big house. He is looked after quite well by his faithful secretary, Khursheed, but his loneliness is his alone, since the demise of his life partner, Shobha.

He is still working. The thought of retiring has never occured to him. He says, 'Acting gives one a feeling of agelessness, of pep and vigour.' Yes, he is very regular and still active. But that does not relieve him of his loneliness. And when he is seated, all alone, memories come back to him, memories of the dear ones who have left him forever. Memories, above all, of Shobha.

There are moments when he feels her presence. Invisible Shobha wanders through the house, sits opposite to him, goes into the kitchen where she used to cook, stoops over the railings of the balcony. She whispers, she sighs, she laughs, she descends the stairs, goes into the garden, loiters for a while and then comes back and flits around him. It is like the holy apparition of the mythical Sita, as described by the Sanskrit dramatist Bhavabhuti in *Uttar Ram Charit*, after her disappearance in the wombs of the earth. Rama loiters in the garden, sad and lonely; Sita's spirit appears and flits around her lord and love, Rama.

But loneliness is also a gift—it helps the wise to grow wiser, the sensitive artistes to grow poetic, to turn into philosophers. And Ashok Kumar is all that. He is a wonderful specimen of humanity, almost perfect.

But Ashok is not religious. He does not believe in it, for according to him, no religion in practice reaches its goal of tolerance and love.

Someone asked him, 'How do you define life, Dadamoni?'

'Life,' Ashok Kumar replied, 'is an unquenchable thirst.'

'And what about God?' the person asked again.

Ashok said, 'I do not know what is God. None can trace out a black cat on a newmoon night.'

The man raised his eyebrows, 'Do you mean to say that you do not believe in anything, Dadamoni?'

Ashok Kumar smiled as he said, 'I believe in Karma. My friend, Krishna has said—*Karmanyeva adhikaraste ma phaleshu kadachana*—you have only the right to do your best; it is not for you to aspire to the fruits of your labour. That is the last word.'

And that is the last word for Ashok Kumar, the legendary Indian who believes in the words of his friend Krishna.

AFTERWORD

Bombay Talkies to Bollywood: The Legend of Dadamoni

'Please do not ask me to embrace the heroine': Ashok Kumar Ganguly had laid this condition to Himanshu Rai when the director of Bombay Talkies had cast him in *Jeevan Naiya*. He tried to wriggle out of the job. When he faced the camera, there was no sparkle in his eyes, he shook his head too much, didn't know what to do with his hands. In fact he was so clumsy before the camera that a co-actor fractured his leg because of him! Who would have thought that one day the same Ashok Kumar would serve as a textbook for actors wanting to perfect characterisation, voice control, timing, gestures, postures? For, the way he lifted his eyes, waved his hand or puffed on his cigarette, breathed life into the personas. He thus transformed the acting style in Indian cinema from Theatrical to Naturalistic—which is still the cinema language worldwide.

Once *Jeevan Naiya* released, everyone, including the Maharaja Scindia of Gwalior, liked the six-feet-tall actor with a nice nose and a habit of talking while laughing. And the same year, 1936, when *Achhut Kanya* hit the screen, the entire subcontinent was swept off its feet. At a time when movie had turned talkie, it was hailed for its call for an egalitarian society, free of the curse of barriers and discriminations based on castes. It had other attractions: a powerful storyline, an enticing pair in the lead roles, and extremely hummable songs. So, in spite of the remote effeminacy that trailed his voice, everyone wanted to listen to '*Main banki chidiyaan*' again and again. Before long, his youngest sibling Kishore started charging listeners for mimicking his Dadamoni!

Achhut Kanya had firmed up Ashok Kumar's resolve to make a mark as an actor worthy of co-starring with the ravishing beauty Devika Rani. He was cast only because the lead actor of Bombay Talkies was absconding but surely he had the makings of a screen actor. So, despite his diffidence, the debutant's simplicity spoke louder than the sophistication of the England-returned heroine. And for six decades after that, the thespian continued to charm the fathers, mothers, sons, daughters and grandchildren of his contemporaries. 'Look, my fans are growing younger!' joked the man who lent a new face to the sobriquet 'Evergreen'.

'To reach perfection, everyone has to go up the stairs step by step,' Rai had said to his protégé. The actor took the lesson to heart and rose in life—to become the director of Bombay Talkies, a shareholder of Filmistan Studios, to set up Ashok Kumar Productions. Yet, till the end of his life, he took his job as an actor earnestly. He would rehearse his lines before a mirror, watch Hollywood films, look at scenes as if they were happening in his household. This personalised the experience for viewers. In *Mahal*, where the persona is always following an illusion, he adapted a different rhythm, a delivered the dialogues very slowly as if he were speaking in a trance. And once he tasted the rasa of merging with a persona, he did not shy of proving his range by playing thief (*Kismet*), old man (*Aashirwad*), killer (*Jewel Thief*), or lech (*Shaukeen*). 'How can you play such a character at your station, Papa?' his daughters had asked the thespian, then a septuagenarian. He had replied, 'There ought to be a surprise element every time you come on the screen, no?'

Thus the evergreen actor kept reinventing himself—and his popularity grew beyond his own imagination. A monk who falls in love with a courtesan (*Chitralekha*). A sadhu who gets away with conning (*Savera*). A zamindar who fights social injustice (*Aashirwad*). An idealistic doctor who ends up killing a molester (*Haatey Bajarey*). A husband who steers his wife away from infidelity (*Gumraah*). An innocent man sent to the gallows (*Kanoon*). A house surgeon in love with a colleague (*Hospital*)—Ashok Kumar became all this. *Mahal, Parineeta, Afsana, Kanoon, Howrah Bridge, Chalti Ka Naam Gaadi, Bandini, Oonchey Log, Haatey Bajarey, Mamta, Pakeezah, Guddi, Chhoti Si Baat, Victoria No. 203, Khatta Meetha, Shaukeen*; ghost stories, romantic love, courtroom dramas, family entertainers, Muslim socials, thrillers, lost-and-found formulas, dirty stories—Dadamoni became the prototype for genre after genre.

'I'm not tempted by awards, but I am by roles,' he once said to Hrishikesh Mukherjee. The directors of the 300-plus films he acted in comprise a who's who of Indian cinema: Mehboob Khan, Nitin Bose, Phani Majumdar, Satyen Bose, Bimal Roy, B.R. Chopra, Kamal Amrohi, Hrishikesh Mukherjee, Shakti Samanta, Vijay Anand. His heroines kept changing: from Devika Rani, Leela Chitnis, Kanan Devi and Nalini Jaywant to Madhubala, Meena Kumari, Nargis, Vyjayantimala, Mala Sinha and Nanda to Nutan, Waheeda Rehman, Suchitra Sen, Saira Banu, Sharmila Tagore, to Hema Malini, Mausami Chatterjee, Jaya Bhaduri and Rekha. His one rule in life seemed to be 'break the rule'.'

This dictum furthered every branch of Indian cinema. The young man—who had given up law when Rai was 'recruiting' educated men from Kolkata—gave a platform to litterateurs like Saadat Hasan Manto, Ismat Chughtai, Shaheed Latif, Kamal Amrohi, Saradindu Bandopadhyay, Premendra Mitra and Nabendu Ghosh, to introduce complex social reality in cinematic storytelling. It enhanced the respectability and acceptability of the pantheon of directors he platformed. He introduced Dilip

Kumar in *Jwar Bhata* and Dev Anand in *Ziddi*, the movie which gave listeners a singer named Kishore Kumar.

A raconteur par excellence in personal life, this Renaissance man practised homeopathy for forty-five years. His leisure hours were spent painting, which, for him, was an expression of feelings. Above all, he was a staunch believer in national and communal integration. 'Artists,' he believed, 'are neither Hindus nor Muslims.' His name, shorn of caste or class connotations, signified this. Much like the proverbial banyan tree, he grew roots at every turn of Bollywood. Raj Kapoor, Dilip Kumar, Dev Anand—the legendary trio held him in reverence. For, at a time when the word 'hero' was synonymous with 'chocolate boy', he essayed characters with moral weakness.

There was a grandeur in Ashok Kumar's stardom that did not rest on publicity. For, unlike today's actors, film stars of yore were not faces seen every ten minutes in any home with a television. But Dadamoni was the first actor to be seen in newspaper advertisements. And when *Hum Log* entered the nation's life, he became a household figure. India's first soap opera, *Hum Log* was our first experiment in development communication, and Doordarshan wanted an anchor who would be universally accepted by viewers across the subcontinent. The 'granddad' of Indian acting fitted the bill so well that soon the postman was delivering gunnybags full of mails at Ashok Kumar's residence. Viewers sought his advise on family planning as well as on the smallest of problems disturbing their domestic peace. Probably this—more than his Filmfare and National Awards, Phalke or Padmashris—made him the subject of a doctoral study in an American university.

The Bolly Family Tree

Some personalities are not curbed by years, they can be measured only by generations. Ashok Kumar, to me, epitomizes this. I'd say he is the one personality who symbolizes Indian Cinema's journey from Bombay Talkies to Bollywood. And there are many windows to view this.

Let's start at the very beginning—with Sashadhar Mukherjee. Husband of Ashok Kumar's sister Sati, he was Dadamoni's anchor in Bombay and his 'go-to' person all along: when he joined as Lab Assistant; when he was forced to become a hero; when Devika Rani shut him out in favour of Amiya Chakravarty. Naturally, when S. Mukherjee left to start Filmistan, Ashok Kumar stepped away too.

This was to prove a milestone in his turning into a thespian—and becoming the 'Elder Brother' of the industry. While Filmistan was to launch many a director, actor and actress, Ashok Kumar was to prove he was bigger than the production house, be it Filmistan or Bombay Talkies. He acted in Mehboob Khan's *Najma* and *Humayun* and they became phenomenal hits. Filmistan was launched with the superhit *Chal Chal Re Naujawan*. The subsequent years saw him make a dramatic return to Bombay Talkies; and Filmistan saw his cousins, nephews and grandnieces all become popular faces of the Hindi-film screen.

S. Mukherjee established his own brothers in every branch of the film industry. But by many accounts, his most enduring contribution to Indian cinema is establishing his wife's brother. His family, that had nothing to do with business, went on to become Showbiz Moguls. His younger brother, Subodh, rose to fame as director of *Munimji, Paying Guest, Junglee, Love Marriage, April Fool, Shagird*; and Prabodh Mukherjee as the producer of those movies. His elder brother, Ravindramohan, did little in films but Ravindramohan's son, Ram Mukherjee, took to direction and his granddaughter Rani Mukherji peaked as an actress. Her tying the knot with Aditya Chopra connects Ashok Kumar with the fabled Chopras—the clan whose head, Baldev Raj, rose to fame with the blessings of Ashok Kumar.

This is just the first generation. Sashadhar and Sati Devi were blessed with five sons and one daughter. The eldest, Rono, directed and composed music for *Tu Hi Meri Zindagi* (1965), featuring his brother Deb Mukherjee, who later starred in films such as *Sambandh, Aansoo Ban Gaye Phool, Ek Bar Muskura Do, Main Tulsi Tere Aangan Ki* and *Baton Baton Mein*. Joy Mukherjee rose to be 'the heartthrob of 1960s' with hits such as *Love in Shimla, Love in Tokyo, Phir Wohi Dil Laya Hoon, Ek Musafir Ek Haseena, Shagird, Humsaya* and *Ziddi* (1964) to his credit.

His fourth son, director Shomu Mukherjee, married renowned actress Tanuja, thus connecting Ashok Kumar to her legendary sister, Nutan; their mother Shobhna Samarth, the remarkable actress in *Hamari Beti, Ram Rajya, Bharat Milap, Chhalia* and *Love in Shimla*; and to her mother Rattan Bai, a popular singer who played Shivaji's mother in *Swarajyacha Seemewar*.

S. Mukherjee's fifth son Shubir and daughter Shibani Maulik are not renowned but the kin-dom kept growing with the third generation. Deb's son Ayan Mukherjee directed *Yeh Jawani Hai Diwani* (2013), while his daughter Sunita married director Ashutosh Gowarikar. Shomu and Tanuja's daughters are the actresses, Kajol and Tanisha; and when Kajol married Ajay Devgn, his father, action director Veeru Devgan, too entered into the Mukherjee-Ganguli fold.

After Ashok Kumar bought up the ownership of Bombay Talkies and returned to helm the institution founded by Himanshu Rai, he introduced his first cousin Arun Mukherjee as playback singer and music director. He had composed music for *Pratima*, the thespian Dilip Kumar's second film, and eventually for *Parineeta*, the first venture of Ashok Kumar Productions. Dadamoni inducted his own sibling Kishore Kumar who rose to legendary heights as singer, actor, writer, director and composer. Kishore Kumar's four marriages linked Dadamoni to actresses Ruma Guha Thakurta, Madhubala, Yogita Bali and Leena Chandavarkar. Kishore Kumar's son from his first marriage, Amit Kumar, carries forward the family's talent in music—perhaps because he also inherited Ruma Guha Thakurta's musical genes. She was the founder of the Calcutta Youth Choir, besides playing remarkable lead and character roles in celebrated Bengali films such as *Nirjan Saikatey* and *Arogya Niketan*.

Dadamoni's links also include Nalini Jaywant, who was a cousin of Shobhna Samarth. And Chhaya Devi—the extremely talented actress who was trained in music by K.C. Dey and in dance—was his aunt through his wife Shobha Rani. After all this, it might sound ironic to see Bharti Jaffrey's words: 'Papa did not want me to be in films and in deference to his wishes I did not take to acting.' Ironic, because genes led Bharti to do theatre with Pearl Padamsee; act in *Saans*, the television serial directed by actress Neena Gupta; face the camera in the films *Devi Ahilya Bai*, *My Pot of Gold*, *Marry Me*, and bring home an award in the seventh decade of her life! By then, her daughter Anuradha Patel had gained national and international recognition through films like *Utsav*, *Ijaazat* and *Jaane Tu Ya Jaane Na*. She is married to Kanwaljit Singh, the actor who captured the nation's imagination with Doordarshan's *Buniyaad* and featured in numerous Hindi and Punjabi films. And Bharti herself had married Hamid Jaffrey, elder brother of the internationally renowned actor Saeed Jaffrey. Does that make Ashok Kumar a 'great granduncle' of the actress Kiara Advani, who is Hamid Jaffrey's granddaughter?

Dadamoni's objection to his daughters joining films stretched to his second daughter Rupa, too, who married Deven Verma, the actor whose comic timing made films such as *Gol Maal*, *Angoor*, *Besharam*, *Khatta Meetha* and *Anupama* enjoyable. But when it came to his third daughter, Preeti, the ban gave way. She trained at FTII and had a short-lived but impressive career that is most cherished in Freni Sethna of *Khatta Meetha*. This film virtually became a 'home movie' as his son Aroop Ganguly went behind the camera to assist Basu Chatterjee. Unlike S. Mukherjee, Dadamoni did not create opportunities for his son to become an actor.

Big Brother

More than any of these relationships, Dadamoni is and will be most remembered as the older brother of Kishore Kumar. His relationship with him was almost fatherly since 'Aabhas', as this sibling was christened, came twenty years after him. Even Anoop was fifteen years younger. Dadamoni was the banyan that arched over them all, but he probably had a special corner for the enormously gifted sibling who inherited their mother's musical genes and their father's funny bones. His vocal skill proved inimitable—be it his yoddling or the song from *Half Ticket*, '*Aake Seedhi Lagi*', rendered in both male and female voice. Like their cousin Arun Mukherjee, Kishore scored for films—*Jhumroo* for one. Like Dadamoni, he acted in films about social upliftment like *Naukri* and *Dhobi Doctor* (both, incidentally, scripted by Nabendu Ghosh) and in laugh riots like *Padosan*, *Half Ticket* and *Lukochuri* (the Bengali classic in which Nabendu Ghosh teamed with Anoop Kumar to create an unforgettable comic character). Additionally, with *Door Gagan Ki Chhaon Mein*, Kishore proved himself as a director—an ambition that had prompted Dadamoni to trade his Law examination fees for a ticket to Bombay...

During his early years in tinsel town, Kishore was in and out of Dadamoni's home. Along with Bharati, Rupa, Aroop and Palu he would wait for the superstar to come home, have a bath, and gather everyone on the terrace of the Kala Ghoda house. There Dadamoni would talk to them, exchange ideas, and cook up O Henry-type stories. He would soon forget the fantastic tales but as he narrated them his children would listen wide-eyed and interject in disbelief—'Really?' Much of the impact was created by 'Kishore Kaka' who would sit at the piano and provide background music. For a sad story he would play a tearful strain and the kids would start crying; for a happy note he would go tara-rum-pum-pum, making everyone clap and dance.

Underlining this playful relationship was a deep respect for Dadamoni, whose grave image was the opposite of Kishore's. But

Dadamoni would say, 'Kishore how do you do all these pranks?' And he would reply, 'You want to do these pranks?' 'Yes, let's!' That's how *Chalti Ka Naam Gaadi* happened, where the elder brother typically scolds the younger brothers but also covers up for their capers. This film truly reflects the equation between the three siblings: fun-loving, jovial, always teasing one another.

Satyen Bose's film revolves around a frustrated lover who resents women so much that he forbids his brothers to marry. Kishore expected it to flop, instead it became a megahit, received favourable reviews for comic situations and musical treatment, and became a cult classic. It reinstated not only Ashok Kumar's box office draw; along with *Phagun*, *Howrah Bridge* and *Kala Paani* it was the fourth hit in 1958 for Madhubala, the child artiste whom Ashok Kumar had led into limelight with her first adult role in *Mahal*.

Chalti Ka Naam Gaadi may have played 'matchmaker' between Kishore and Madhubala before they tied the knot in 1960. Kishore later made two take offs on it: *Badhti Ka Naam Dadhi* in 1974 and *Chalti Ka Naam Zindagi* in 1981, with diminishing returns. These too featured the three brothers. *Badhti Ka Naam Dadhi* was a mayhem around a millionaire who decides to leave his wealth to the man who grows the longest beard, while *Chalti Ka Naam Zindagi* brought in Amit Kumar through a jaded story about two brothers trying to reunite their bade bhaiyya with his estranged wife and son, running into trouble with a villain out to retrieve his loot from a well on which their hotel is built.

In real life, Dadamoni would badger his chota bhai, '*Tum toh bade Mohabbat Khan ban gaye Bhai—char char biwiyaan*! Quite the Casanova—four wives! And I have spent my life with just one!' He would even address his brother as 'Mohabbat Khan'. Perhaps he knew that their father had, many moons ago, drawn his youngest son's birth-chart and predicted that 'he will marry four times to find marital happiness.' The prediction proved true as Kishore married Ruma Ghosh (Guha Thakurta after her second marriage), Begum Mumtaz Jahan Dehlavi (Madhubala), Yogita Bali (later married to Mithun Chakravarty) and finally settled with Leena Chandavarkar (who was widowed by the accidental death of her first husband, Siddharth Bandodkar). With his first and his fourth wife, Kishor Kumar had two sons, Amit and Sumit. Though all his wives were actresses, and Kishore himself had proven his acting capability, his sons did not take to acting. Amit Kumar is a recognised singer who is currently involved in the making of a biopic on his legendary father.

At Home

The humane face of the actor comes through most vividly in this account by Dr Ratna Mukherjee, who was HOD of Psychology at Tilka Manjhi Bhagalpur University, Bhagalpur. She is the daughter of Arun Kumar Mukherjee—Ashok Kumar's first cousin—and is still adored in the song '*Gorey gorey haathon mein mehdi lagaa ke*' from *Parineeta*. 'My dadi and Bharti Didi's dadi were sisters. The elder sister Luna, also known as Gauri Rani, had three sons—the Kumar brothers; and my grandmother Bina had only one—my father. She passed away when baba was only three months old, so he was raised mostly by Dadamoni's mother who'd say, "I have four sons…" Baba was no less than a son to her.

'Baba had a massive heart attack while driving a car and passed away when he was just forty-two. Maa was a young widow with two little daughters: Bandana, a.k.a Benu, and I, Ratu. Since then Ashok Kumar would send money every single month for our education, wellness, Didi's marriage—everything. He helped us find our bearings in the world. Didi completed her Master's. After getting my doctorate I became a professor and rose to the post of proctor of the University.

'In 1987 we visited Bombay when Kishore Kaka passed away. I told Jethumoni, "Now I have started earning, you don't send money to Maa." With one look from head to foot he sized me up, "I didn't know you have grown so big…" Even today, I wither when I remember that look of his. If I were to place Ashok Kumar on an altar, I will bow to him before I do to any deity. No one has seen god—I have, in the form of Jethumoni.'

This face of the thespian was not confined to home. He was same elder brother to people in Bombay Talkies. At the Ashok Kumar Centenary, which I curated for the Tapan Sinha Foundation at Nandan-West Bengal Film Centre in 2011, Shakti Samanta had recounted how, after he joined as assistant director to Phani Majumdar, he had expressed his desire to become an actor. Dadamoni had advised him that he should take up direction instead. Perhaps Ashok Kumar saw a bit of himself in the young man: he would often ask Shakti to play small roles, generally as a policeman. Some years down when Shakti got a chance to direct *Inspector*, he approached Dadamoni to play the lead. '*Toh tu mujhse badla le raha hai*!' he responded, 'This is your revenge for me casting *you* as policemen!' The 1956 film proved a hit and, till the end, Ashok Kumar remained the first to be cast by the director in all his movies. The first film produced by Shakti Films would be a challenge since he could not afford the then reigning pair of Ashok Kumar and Madhubala. He told Dadamoni this even before he narrated the story. Once he heard Shakti out, Dadamoni magnanimously signed the contract for Re 1, saying, 'I will collect my payment when the film is released.' Dadamoni even persuaded Madhubala's father to let her act in it, and when Shakti narrated the story to her on the sets of *Mughal-e-Azam*, she agreed to act in *Howrah Bridge* on the same terms as Ashok Kumar.

Funny Dadamoni

The climax of *Howrah Bridge* was to show Ashok Kumar chase the villain to the top of the bridge and fight him there. Full of mischief, the thespian cooked up an excuse to avoid climbing the bridge: '*Shakti yaar, main hero hoon, main kyon villain ke pichhe*

pichhe jaoon? Instead of chasing the the villain, I will wait right here. He will climb down when he feels hungry, or wants to pee, and I will push him off the bridge into the Ganga.' 'But you are the hero!' Shakti remonstrated. 'If you were in the audience, would you like to see the hero wait for the villain to climb down to pee?' Without waiting for Shakti to finish, Dadamoni rose to give the shot.

I witnessed this mazakiya—funny—side of Dadamoni in 1979, on the sets of *Chalti Ka Naam Zindagi*. I was a cub reporter with *Screen* which then had B.K. Karanjia as its editor. All three Kumars—Kishore, Anoop and Ashok—were overjoyed to learn that I was the daughter of, as they respectively addressed him, 'Nabendu Da', 'Nabendu', 'Mr Braken'! 'Who's that?' I asked, startled by this new identity of my father. Dadamoni laughed uproariously as he demystified me with a flashback.

In 1952, Nabendu and Arabind Sen had gone with Dadamoni to Matheran where his family was holidaying. In the evening they started discussing an adaptation of Oliver Goldsmith's novel *The Vicar of Wakefield*. When night fell and whisky was served, Baba politely said, 'Cigarette is my only addiction, Dadamoni.' Ashok Kumar asked him, 'You haven't sworn by any deity not to touch alcohol, have you? If not, have a little, it will add flavour to your narrative.' But Dadamoni's 'little' was a little too much and Baba lost control of his tongue as the story reached the climax. He said: 'The villagers led by the hero saw that the zamindar's bedroom door was shut, locked from within. Agitated by this, they banged furiously And the door was *braken*...' Ever since, Baba was 'Mr Braken' for Dadamoni just as Kishore Kumar was 'Mohabbat Khan'.

Humour came naturally to the grand figure, as Mausumi Chatterjee narrates: 'The first thing he told me at my wedding was, "*Tu toh abhi bhi balika badhu hai*, so why this hurry to marry when I am still around?"'

Dadamoni was in his element when he played naughty,

mischievous, wicked characters. Perhaps that is why not a single remake of his fun films—*Shaukeen*, *Khoobsurat* or *Victoria No. 203*—succeeded.

Virtuoso Performance

When Ashok Kumar was cast in *Jeevan Naiya*, his engagement was called off by the bride's father. Funny? No, it was cruel. It was a reflection on the way society perceived actors then, as Dadamoni had explained in a conversation with Nabendu: 'Once upon a time actors and dancers were social outcasts even though everyone enjoyed their performance.' And in 1940s, when actors gained popularity and social acceptance, the tradition-bound Indian society still said, 'Ghor Kaliyug! Apocalyse now. That's why everything is going topsy turvy...' Nevertheless, it was as an actor that Ashok Kumar achieved everything in life—fame, money, legendary stature.

In my preteens, I would visit the family at their six-storeyed mansion in the upscale neighbourhood of Kala Ghoda in Mumbai. In later years, when I joined Elphinstone College, this house was home to the iconic music store Rhythm House, until 2016. Much later I learnt that this building had helped Ashok Kumar salvage Bombay Talkies after Devika Rani married Svetoslav Roerich and left the institution to flounder.

Dadamoni had bought the property from an Englishman who owned S. Rose and Co., which did business in piano, music manuscript and records. After Independence the Englishman went back to England. When the company's accounts were settled, Ashok Kumar was credited with 11,000 pounds. That fortune helped in buying Bombay Talkies when it went into liquidation.

~

Ashok Kumar was the first actor to face censorship, in the movie *Sangram*. Prior to that he came close to it with the song '*Door hato ae duniyawalon Hindustan hamara hain.*' Kavi Pradeep's lyrics, rendered by Arun Mukherjee along with a chorus, was content fit for the scissors in British India, especially when the 'Quit India!' slogan had been unleashed. The song was picturised against a map of India and the words went '*Shuru hua hain jung tumhara jaag utho Hindustani...* (Your struggle has just started, do not relent O people of Hindustan)'. Did they get away with it because Ashok Kumar was an anti-hero? Or, was it the compromise lent by the following lines: '*Tum na kisi ke aage jhukna, German ho ya Japani* (Don't you relent before any force, be they German or Japanese)'?

~

Dadamoni had a signature style of holding the cigarette. Initially, it was because he did not know what to do with his hands—they felt so awkward, he felt self-conscious. Then, when he started studying the Hollywood actors, he zeroed in on Humphrey Bogart and mastered his ease. He used the prop very subtly—'It must not distract the viewer from the main action,' he'd remind himself. Somewhere along the line he started smoking almost fifty cigarettes a day, but, thankfully he did not suffer like Bimal Roy, who succumbed to throat cancer at fifty-six.

~

Dadamoni had no fear of becoming 'common' by appearing in advertisements, or on television. In the beginning, when there was only the print medium, he was seen in advertisements for Brylcreem, Prudent toothpaste, suit lengths. On television though, he is most remembered for the Pan Parag ad he did with Shammi Kapoor. This ad film was a dream come true for the *Junglee* actor, who by this time had grown in years as well as girth, to fit the persona of a groom's father. And Dadamoni played the bride's father who's relieved when the 'samdhi' demands not dowry but the branded Pan Masala.

This ad with a subtle anti-dowry message garnered such a huge recall value that even in distant Hong Kong and Europe people would chime Preeti Sagar's jingle when they sighted the 1960s superstar—leading Shammi to be pulled up by his elder brother, showman Raj Kapoor. 'But how could I tell him that I did this ad as it was my only chance to appear in a film with Ashok Kumar—the star of my life, my idol since childhood, the finest actor in India whom I have been a fan of since I was a kid?' he had said in *Shammi Kapoor Unplugged*, going on to add: 'Dadamoni to me was the kind of actor I should have become. My god! What an actor!'

~

Then there was the world of television serials. The rap Dadamoni performed as the Sutradhar made the nonsense rhyme 'Chhand pakaiya' a household word in late 1980s. Twenty-five years later, Diana Mathias, then a young media professional, had said that 'his name immediately conjures the couplet and limericks he used to sign off *Hum Log* with.' Yes, it was pathbreaking but Dadamoni was not one to rest on laurels. Fond of Vijay Anand as a director, he co-acted with him in a fifty-two-episode crime drama series, *Tehkikaat* wherein two private detectives embark on different quests to solve murder mysteries. On Doordarshan he also acted in *Bahadur Shah Zafar* for B.R. Chopra, at the end of which he had only one comment: 'Not in my whole career have I spoken so much Urdu!'

~

Dadamoni would study not only his characters, he would closely observe his co-actors: how they sat, how they moved, how they cast their glance, how they reacted when he spoke. He observed even his patients. And he used his observation for paintings as much as for acting. 'It is so difficult to make it look so easy,' he would say.

Passion was the key to his performance. An incident on the sets of *Humayun* exemplifies this. He was in Rajasthan for the shooting of the Mehboob Khan film. There were thirty to forty horses on set for a war sequence. Suddenly one went berserk and the others followed him. Humayun, being a Muslim, was kneeling on the ground for a sejda when the mayhem ensued. But Dadamoni sat still through it all while the horses stampeded past him and over him too. On the verge of suffering a heart attack, Mehboob Khan's first thought was, 'How will I face the country if something happened to Ashok Kumar!' By god's grace, the star was unscathed—a fact the director attributed to his being in a state of grace.

~

Dadamoni did have a streak of a philosopher in him. When Manto migrated to Pakistan rejecting all his pleas, he was crestfallen. The Urdu writer was, after all, a friend with whom he could share his wonderful ideas for social reform. But he took it in his stride, just as he did when he was outrageously cheated by people he trusted and had to close down Bombay Talkies. 'This must be my Karma,' he'd say, 'I must have owed him something in a previous life!' Besides, '*Paisa aayega toh paisa jayega bhi,* what comes in will go out too,' he'd repeat. His ultimate words? 'My friend Krishna has taught me that work is all I can do—the result of my action is not for me to worry about!'

So, his one and only regret in life was: 'If only I could play the sort of characters Hollywood actors do!' Yet, calls from David Lean to act in Hollywood films left him cold. The director of *Lawrence of Arabia, Ryan's Daughter, Dr Zhivago* was among the honourable guests at the first Republic Day parade in Delhi in 1950, as was Ashok Kumar. The two legends struck a lasting friendship that saw the Hollywood director trying to get the Indian actor to feature in some American movies. Dadamoni refused saying, 'I am an Indian and I am good for Indians. I have no ambition to conquer the world.' His main reservation came from his aversion to being typecast as a stereotypical 'Indian': he felt he would not be cast in a role that would make any difference whatsoever.

~

Of course, within the country he had a surfeit of adulation. So much so that his daughters could never get him on his phone. As a child, Bharti would often cut off callers saying, 'Wrong number!' But after her mother passed away, when she wanted to contact her Papa in Chembur before she set out from her home in Cuffe Parade, she would be exasperated to find the phone constantly engaged. One day she accosted him when she found the phone off the hook. 'Put it back in place,' he told her with twinkling eyes. She did, and forthwith the phone rang. Someone wanted him to be the chief guest. An earnest invitation to a son's wedding. 'Dadamoni, please, just two minutes!' 'Sir this function can't be held without you.' 'Please help me out...' 'Please talk to so-n-so' Producers, directors, actors, patients, people in need, socialites— the phone kept ringing, *constantly*! Until she took it off the hook again.

The Ashok Kumar Foundation

Being an institution by himself, the actor who spanned decades between 1936 and 1999 left a priceless legacy for generations to follow. To share that with everybody, Bharti Jaffrey set up the Ashok Kumar Foundation (AKF). Furthering his attachment to homeopathy, the charitable organisation donated medicines to a clinic that cared for deprived children. It also raised funds through events to be donated for relief work and other philanthropic causes. AKF funded noteworthy scripts—the first recipient of which was *Shwaas*, the Marathi film that won the National award before going to the Oscars in 2004. It also actively supported new theatre groups and upcoming artists—and this started with a fascinating incident.

One afternoon, the doorbell rang. 'Speedpost,' said the man at the door. While Bharti was signing the delivery sheet, the postman asked, 'Ma'am is that painting by Paul Raj?' This was the artist from whom Ashok Kumar had mastered the art of painting in watercolour—the most difficult medium as it permits no alteration—without pencilling an outline. Stunned, the daughter asked, 'How did you recognise the signature?' The courier revealed that he had joined J.J. College of Art in Bombay but didn't have the money to continue. In that instant, she resolved to help debuting artists in mounting shows, bringing out brochures—and sharing space with Dadamoni's art.

Today, AKF has folded its umbrella. Its request to the most popular film award to institute one in the name of the man who lived and breathed to ensure that Indian Cinema lived and breathed, has gone unheeded. A postal stamp is all that remains to commemorate the man who deserves the gratitude of every Indian viewer for giving us a cinema that upholds every Indian ideal, from brotherhood of man to work is worship.

With this book, I bow once more to the legend who took Indian Cinema from Bombay Talkies to Bollywood.

Ratnottama Sengupta

Filmography

1936
Achhut Kanya
Dir: Franz Osten
Music: Saraswati Devi
With: Devika Rani

Janma Bhoomi
Dir: Franz Osten
Music: Saraswati Devi
With: Devika Rani

Jeevan Naiya
Dir: Franz Osten
Music: Saraswati Devi
With: Devika Rani

1937
Izzat
Dir: Franz Osten
Music: Saraswati Devi
With: Devika Rani

Prem Kahani
Dir: Franz Osten
Music: Saraswati Devi
With: Maya Devi, Madhurika

Savitri
Dir: Franz Osten
Music: Saraswati Devi
With: Devika Rani, Sunita Devi

1938
Nirmala
Dir: Franz Osten
Music: Saraswati Devi
With: Devika Rani

Vachan
Dir: Franz Osten
Music: Saraswati Devi
With: Devika Rani

1939
Kangan
Dir: Franz Osten
Music: Saraswati Devi, Ramchandra Pal
With: Leela Chitnis

1940
Azad
Dir: N.R. Acharya
Music: Saraswati Devi, Ramchandra Pal
With: Leela Chitnis

Bandhan
Dir: N.R. Acharya
Music: Saraswati Devi, Ramchandra Pal
With: Leela Chitnis

1941

Anjaan
Dir: Amiya Chakravarty
Music: Pannalal Ghosh
With: Devika Rani

Jhoola
Dir: Gyan Mukherjee
Music: Saraswati Devi
With: Leela Chitnis

Naya Sansar
Dir: N.R. Acharya
Music: Saraswati Devi, Ramchandra Pal
With: Renuka Devi

1943

Angoothi
Dir: B. Mittra
Music: Prof Deodhar, Ashok Ghosh, Lalubhai Bhojak
With: Chandraprabha

Kismet
Dir: Gyan Mukherjee
Music: Anil Biswas
With: Mumtaz Shanti

Najma
Dir: Mehboob
Music: Rafiq Ghaznavi
With: Veena

1944

Chal Chal Re Naujawan
Dir: Gyan Mukherjee
Music: Ghulam Haider
With: Naseem

Kiran
Dir: Jagirdar
Music: Ninu Mazumdar
With: Leela Chitnis

1945
Begum
Dir: Sushil Mazumdar
Music: H.P. Das
With: Naseem

Humayun
Dir: Mehboob
Music: Ghulam Haider
With: Veena, Nargis

1946
Eight Days
Dir: Dattaram Pai
Music: S.D. Burman
With: Veera

Shikari
Dir: Savak Vachha
Music: S.D. Burman
With: Veera, Paro

1947
Sajan
Dir: Kishore Sahu
Music: C. Ramchandra
With: Rehana

1948
Chandrashekhar
Dir: Debaki Bose
Music: Kamal Das Gupta
With: Kanan Devi

Padmini
Dir: Walli
Music: Ghulam Haider
With: Mumtaz Shanti

1949
Mahal
Dir: Kamal Amrohi
Music: Khemchand Prakash
With: Madhubala

1950
Aadhi Raat
Dir: S.K. Ojha
Music: Husnlal Bhagatram
With: Nargis

Khiladi
Dir: R.C. Talwar
Music: Hansraj Behl
With: Suraiya

Mashal
Dir: Nitin Bose
Music: S.D. Burman, Manna Dey
With: Sumitra Devi, Ruma Devi

Nishana
Dir: Wajahat Mirza
Music: Khurshid Anwar
With: Madhubala, Shyama, Geeta Bali

Samadhi
Dir: Ramesh Saigal
Music: C. Ramchandra
With: Nalini Jaywant

Sangram
Dir: Gyan Mukherjee
Music: C. Ramchandra
With: Nalini Jaywant

1951
Afsana
Dir: B.R. Chopra
Music: Husnlal Bhagatram
With: Veena, Jeevan

Deedar
Dir: Nitin Bose
Music: Naushad
With: Nargis, Dilip Kumar, Nimmi

1952
Betaab
Dir: Harbans
Music: S.D. Batish
With: Motilal, Naseem

Bewafa
Dir: M.L. Anand
Music: A.R. Qureshi
With: Nargis, Raj Kapoor

Jalpari
Dir: Mohan Sinha
Music: Gobindram
With: Nalini Jaywant, Geeta Bali

Kafila
Dir: Arvind Sen
Music: Husnlal Bhagatram
With: Nalini Jaywant

Nau Bahar
Dir: Pt Anand Kumar
Music: Roshan
With: Nalini Jaywant

Poonam
Dir: M. Sadiq
Music: Shankar Jaikishen
With: Kamini Kaushal

Raag Rang
Dir: Digvijay
Music: Roshan
With: Geeta Bali

Saloni
Dir: J.P. Advani
Music: Basant Prakash
With: Nalini Jaywant

Tamasha
Dir: Phani Muzumdar
Music: Khemchand Prakash, Manna Dey
With: Dev Anand, Meena Kumari, Kishore

1953
Nagma
Dir: Nakshab
Music: Naushad
With: Nadira

Parineeta
Dir: Bimal Roy
Music: Arun Kumar
With: Meena Kumari

Shamsheer
Dir: Gyan Mukherjee
Music: Arun Kumar
With: Bhanumati

Shole
Dir: B.R. Chopra
Music: Dhaniram, Naresh Bhattacharya
With: Bina Rai, Purnima

1954

Baadbaan
Dir: Phani Muzumdar
Music: Timir Baran, S.K. Pal
With: Dev Anand, Meena Kumari

Lakeeren
Dir: Harbans
Music: Hafeez Khan
With: Nalini Jaywant

Naaz
Dir: S.K. Ojha
Music: Anil Biswas
With: Nalini Jaywant, Veena

Samaj
Dir: Vasant Joglekar
Music: Arun Kumar
With: Shashikala, Usha Kiran

1955

Bandish
Dir: Satyen Bose
Music: Hemant Kumar
With: Meena Kumari, Daisy Irani

Sardar
Dir: Gyan Mukherjee
Music: Jagmohan
With: Bina Rai

1956
Bhai Bhai
Dir: M.V. Raman
Music: Madan Mohan
With: Kishore Kumar, Nimmi, Nirupa Roy

Ek Hi Rasta
Dir: B.R. Chopra
Music: Hemant Kumar
With: Meena Kumari, Sunil Dutt

Inspector
Dir: Shakti Samanta
Music: Hemant Kumar
With: Geeta Bali

Shatranj
Dir: Gyan Mukherjee
Music: C Ramchandra
With: Meena Kumari

1957
Bandi
Dir: Satyen Bose
Music: Hemant Kumar
With: Bina Rai, Kishore Kumar

Ek Saal
Dir: Devendra Goel
Music: Ravi
With: Madhubala

Jeevan Sathi
Dir: R.S. Tara
Music: Bulo C. Rani
With: Usha Kiron

Mr. X
Dir: Nanabhai Bhatt
Music: N. Dutta
With: Nalini Jaywant

Sheroo
Dir: Shakti Samanta
Music: Madan Mohan
With: Nalini Jaywant

Talaash
Dir: Vishram Bedekar
Music: C. Ramchandra
With: Bina Rai, Ameeta

Ustad
Dir: Nanabhai Bhatt
Music: O.P. Nayyar
With' Anjali Devi, Anita Guha

1958
Chalti Ka Naam Gaadi
Dir: Satyen Bose
Music: S.D. Burman
With: Veena, Madhubala, Kishore Kumar, Anoop Kumar

Farishta
Dir: Ravindra Dave
Music: O.P. Nayyar
With: Sohrab Modi, Meena Kumari

Howrah Bridge
Dir: Shakti Samanta
Music: O.P. Nayyar
With: Madhubala

Karigar
Dir: Vasant Joglekar
Music: C. Ramchandra
With: Nirupa Roy

Light House
Dir: G.P. Sippy
Music: N. Dutta
With: Nutan

Night Club
Dir: Naresh Saigal
Music: Madan Mohan
With: Kamini Kaushal

Ragini
Dir: Rakhan
Music: O.P. Nayyar
With: Kishore Kumar, Padmini

Savera
Dir: Satyen Bose
Music: Sailesh Mukherjee
With: Meena Kumari

Sitaron Se Aage
Dir: Sayen Bose
Music: S.D. Burman
With: Vyjayantimala

1959
Baap Bete
Dir: Raja Paranjpe
Music: Madan Mohan
With: Shyama, Chitra

Bedard Zamana Kya Jane
Dir: Babubhai Mistry
Music: Kalyanji Anandji
With: Nirupa Roy

Daaka
Dir: Nanabhai Bhatt
Music: Chitragupt
With: Nirupa Roy

Dhool Ka Phool
Dir: Yash Chopra
Music: N. Dutta
With: Rajendra Kumar, Mala Sinha

Kangan
Dir: Nanabhai Bhatt
Music: Chitragupta
With: Nirupa Roy

Naach Ghar
Dir: R.S. Tara
Music: N Dutta
With: Shobha Khote

Nai Rahen
Dir: Brij Sadanah
Music: Ravi
With: Geeta Bali

1960
Aanchal
Dir: Vasant Joglekar
Music: C. Ramchandra
With: Nirupa Roy, Nanda

Kala Aadmi
Dir: Ved-Madan
Music: Dattaram
With: Shyama

Kalpana
Dir: Rakhan
Music: O.P. Nayyar
With: Padmini, Ragini

Kanoon
Dir: B.R. Chopra
Music: Salil Chowdhury
With: Rajendra Kumar, Nanda

Masoom
Dir: Satyen Bose
Music: Robin Banerjee
With: Sarosh Irani, Honey Irani

Hospital
Dir: Sushil Mazumdar
Music: Amal Mukherjee
With: Suchitra Sen, Pahari Sanyal

1961
Dark Street
Dir: Naresh Saigal
Music: Dattaram
With: Nishi

Flat No. 9
Dir: Ramesh Sharma
Music: Usha Khanna
With: Sayeeda Khan

Warrant
Dir: Kedar Kapoor
Music: Roshan
With: Shakila

1962
Aarti
Dir: Phani Muzumdar
Music: Roshan
With: Meena Kumari, Pradeep Kumar

Bezuban
Dir: Ram Kamlani
Music: Chitragupt
With: Nirupa Roy

Burma Road
Dir: Tara Harish
Music: Chitragupta
With: Sheikh Mukhtar, Kumkum

Hongkong
Dir: Pachhi
Music: O.P. Nayyar
With: B Saroja Devi

Isi Ka Naam Duniya Hai
Dir: Shakti
Music: Ravi
With: Shyama

Mehandi Lagi Mere Haath
Dir: Suraj Prakash
Music: Kalyanji Anandji
With: Nanda, Shashi Kapoor

Naqli Nawab
Dir: Tara Harish
Music: Babul
With: Manoj Kumar, Shakila

Private Secretary
Dir: Chander
Music: D. Dilip
With: Jayshree Gadkar

Rakhi
Dir: A. Bhimsingh
Music: Ravi
With: Waheeda Rehman, Pradeep Kumar

1963
Aaj Aur Kal
Dir: Vasant Joglekar
Music: Ravi
With: Sunil Dutt, Nanda

Bandini
Dir: Bimal Roy
Music: S.D. Burman
With: Nutan, Dharmendra

Grihasthi
Dir: Kishore Sahu
Music: Ravi
With: Nirupa Roy

Gumrah
Dir: B.R. Chopra
Music: Ravi
With: Mala Sinha, Sunil Dutt

Mere Mehboob
Dir: H.S. Rawail
Music: Naushad
With: Rajendra Kumar, Sadhana

Meri Surat Teri Ankehen
Dir: Rakhan
Music: S.D. Burman
With: Pradeep Kumar, Asha Parekh

Ustadon Ke Ustad
Dir: Brij
Music: Ravi
With: Pradeep Kumar, Shakila

Yeh Raaste Hai Pyar Ke
Dir: R.K. Nayyar
Music: Ravi
With: Sunil Dutt, Leela Naidu

1964
Benazir
Dir: S. Khalil
Music: S.D. Burman
With: Meena Kumari, Shashi Kapoor

Chitralekha
Dir: Kedar Sharma
Music: Roshan
With: Meena Kumari, Pradeep Kumar

Dooj Ka Chand
Dir: Nitin Bose
Music: Roshan
With: Bharat Bhushan, B. Saroja Devi

Phoolon Ki Sej
Dir: Inder Raj Anand
Music: P. Adinarayana Rao
With: Vyjantimala, Manoj Kumar

Pooja Ke Phool
Dir: A. Bhim Singh
Music: Madan Mohan
With: Mala Sinha, Dharmendra

1965
Aadhi Raat Ke Baad
Dir: Nanabhai Bhatt
Music: Chitragupta
With: Ragini

Akashdeep
Dir: Phani Muzumdar
Music: Chitragupta
With: Nanda, Dharmendra

Bahu Beti
Dir: T. Prakash Rao
Music: Ravi
With: Mala Sinha, Joy Mukherjee

Bheegi Raat
Dir: Kalidas
Music: Roshan
With: Meena Kumari, Pradeep Kumar

Chand Aur Suraj
Dir: Dulal Guha
Music: Salil Chowdhury
With: Dharmendra, Nirupa Roy

Naya Kanoon
Dir: R.C. Talwar
Music: Madan Mohan
With: Vyjantimala, Bharat Bhushan

Oonchey Log
Dir: Phani Muzumdar
Music: Chitragupta
With: Raaj Kumar, Feroz Khan, K.R. Vijaya

1966

Afsana
Dir: Brij
Music: Chitragupta
With: Pradeep Kumar, Padmini

Daadi Maa
Dir: L.V. Prasad
Music: Roshan
With: Bina Rai

Mamta
Dir: Asit Sen
Music: Roshan
With: Dharmendra, Suchitra Sen

Yeh Zindagi Kitni Haseen Hai
Dir: R.K. Nayyar
Music: Ravi
With: Joy Mukherjee, Saira Banu

1967
Jewel Thief
Dir: Vijay Anand
Music: S.D. Burman
With: Dev Anand, Vyjayantimala

Meherban
Dir: A. Bhim Singh
Music: Ravi
With: Sunil Dutt, Nutan

Nai Roshni
Dir: Sridhar
Music: Ravi
With: Raaj Kumar, Biswajeet, Mala Sinha

1968
Aabroo
Dir: C.L. Rawal
Music: Sonik Omi
With: Vimi, Deepak Kumar

Aashirwad
Dir: Hrishikesh Mukherjee
Music: Vasant Desai
With: Sanjeev Kumar, Sumitra Sanyal

Dil Aur Muhabbat
Dir: Anand Datta
Music: O.P. Nayyar
With: Joy Mukherji, Sharmila Tagore

Ek Kali Muskayee
Dir: Vasant Joglekar
Music: Madan Mohan
With: Joy Mukherji, Meera

1969

Aansoo Ban Gaye Phool
Dir: Satyen Bose
Music: Laxmikant Pyarelal
With: Deb Mukherjee, Alka

Bhai Bahen
Dir: A. Bhim Singh
Music: Shankar Jaikishen
With: Sunil Dutt, Nutan

Do Bhai
Dir: Brij
Music: Laxmikant Pyarelal
With: Mala Sinha, Jeetendra

Inteqam
Dir: R.K. Nayyar
Music: Laxmikant Pyarelal
With: Sadhana, Sanjay Khan

Paisa Ya Pyar
Dir: Javar Sitaraman
Music: Ravi
With: Mala Sinha, Biswajeet

Pyar Ka Sapna
Dir: Hrishikesh Mukherjee
Music: Chitragupta
With: Mala Sinha, Biswajeet

Satyakam
Dir: Hrishikesh Mukherjee
Music: Laxmikant Pyarelal
With: Dharmendra, Sharmila Tagore

AS CHARACTER ARTISTE

1970
Adhikar
Dir: S. Noor
Music: S.M. Sagar
With: Nanda, Deb Mukherjee

Jawab
Dir: Ramanna
Music: Laxmikant Pyarelal
With: Meena Kumari, Jeetendra, Leena Chandravarkar

Maa Aur Mamta
Dir: Asit Sen
Music: Laxmikant Pyarelal
With: Nutan, Jeetendra, Mumtaz

Door Ka Rahi
Dir: Kishore Kumar
Music: Kishore Kumar
With: Kishore Kumar, Tanuja, Amit Kumar, Padma Khanna

Naya Zamana
Dir: Pramod Chakaravarthy
Music: S.D. Burman
With: Dharmendra, Hema Malini, Pran

Purab Aur Paschim
Dir: Manoj Kumar
Music: Kalyanji Anandji
With: Manoj Kumar, Saira Banu, Pran

Safar
Dir: Asit Sen
Music: Kalyanji Anandji
With: Rajesh Khanna, Sharmila Tagore

Sharafat
Dir: Asit Sen
Music: Laxmikant Pyarelal
With: Hema Malini, Dharmendra

1971

Ganga Tera Pani Amrit
Dir: Virendra Sinha
Music: Ravi
With: Rehman, Navin Nischal, Yogeeta Bali

Hum Tum Aur Woh
Dir: Shiv Kumar
Music: Kalyanji Anandji
With: Vinod Khanna, Bharati

Kangan
Dir: K.B. Tilak
Music: Kalyanji Anandji
With: Mala Sinha, Sanjeev Kumar

Umeed
Dir: Nitin Bose
Music: Ravi
With: Joy Mukherjee, Nanda, Leela Naidu

Pakeezah
Dir: Kamal Amrohi
Music: Ghulam Mohammed
With: Meena Kumari, Raaj Kumar, Veena

1972
Anuraag
Dir: Shakti Samanta
Music: S.D. Burman
With: Vinod Mehra, Mousami Chatterjee

Dil Daulat Aur Duniya
Dir: P.N. Arora
Music: Shankar Jaikishan
With: Sadhana, Rajesh Khanna

Maalik
Dir: A. Bhim Singh
Music: Kalyanji Anandji
With: Rajesh Khanna, Sharmila Tagore

Raakhi Aur Hathkadi
Dir: S.M. Sagar
Music: R.D. Burman
With: Asha Parekh, Vijay Arora

Sa-Re-Ga-Ma-Pa
Dir: Satyen Bose
Music: Ganesh
As Guest Artiste
With: Nazneen, Ruby Chauhan

Sazaa
Dir: Chand
Music: Sonik Omi
With: Pran, Yogeeta Bali, Kabir Bedi

Victoria No 203
Dir: Brij
Music: Kalyanji Anandji
With: Saira Banu, Navin Nischal, Pran

Zameen Aasman
Dir: A. Veerappan
Music: Kishore Kumar
With: Sunil Dutt, Rekha, Yogeeta Bali

Zindagi Zindagi
Dir: Tapan Sinha
Music: S.D. Burman
With: Sunil Dutt, Waheeda Rehman

1973
Bada Kabuthar
Dir: Deven Varma
Music: R.D. Burman
With: Rehana Sultan, Nikhilesh, Deven Varma

Dhund
Dir: B.R. Chopra
Music: Ravi
As Guest Artist
With: Zeenat Aman, Sanjay Khan

Do Phool
Dir: S. Ramanathan
Music: R.D. Burman
With: Vinod Mehra, Aruna Irani, Mehmood

Hifazat
Dir: K.S.R. Das
Music: R.D. Burman
As Guest Artist
With: Vinod Mehra, Asha Sachdev

Taxi Driver
Dir: Mohid Hussain
Music: O.P. Nayyar
With: Anupama, Vishal Anand, Helen

1974

Do Aankhen
Dir: Ajay Biswas
Music: Hansraj Behl
With: Biswajeet, Rekha, Deb Mukherjee

Dulhan
Dir: C.V. Rajendran
Music: Laxmikant Pyarelal
With: Jeetendra, Hema Malini

Khoon Ki Kimat
Dir: Shibu Mittra
Music: Sonik Omi
As Guest Artist
With: Mahendra Sandhu, Neelam Mehra

Paise Ki Gudiya
Dir: Brij
Music: Laxmikant Pyarelal
With: Saira Banu, Navin Nischal

Prem Nagar
Dir: K.S. Prakash Rao
Music: S.D. Burman
As Guest Artist
With: Rajesh Khanna, Hema Malini

Ujala Hi Ujala
Dir: S.M. Sagar
Music: R.D. Burman
With: Vinod Mehra, Yogeeta Bali

1975
Aakraman
Dir: J. Om Prakash
Music: Laxmikant Pyarelal
With: Sanjeev Kumar, Rekha

Chhoti Si Baat
Dir: Basu Chatterji
Music: Salil Chowdhury
With: Amol Palekar, Vidya Sinha

Chori Mera Kaam
Dir: Brij
Music: Kalyanji Anandji
With: Shashi Kapoor, Zeenat Aman

Dafaa 302
Dir: Chand
Music: Laxmikant Pyarelal
With: Randhir Kapoor, Rekha

Ek Mahal Sapnon Ka
Dir: Devendra Goel
Music: Ravi
With: Dharmendra, Sharmila Tagore

Mili
Dir: Hrishikesh Mukherjee
Music: S.D. Burman
With: Amitabh Bachchan, Jaya Bhaduri

Uljhan
Dir: Raghunath Jhalani
Music: Kalyanji Anandji
With: Sanjeev Kumar, Sulakshana Pandit

1976
Aap Beetee
Dir: Mohan Kumar
Music: Laxmikant Pyarelal
With: Shashi Kapoor, Hema Malini

Arjun Pandit
Dir: Hrishikesh Mukherjee
Music: S.D. Burman
With: Sanjeev Kumar, Vinod Mehra, Srividya

Barood
Dir: Pramod Chakravarthy
Music: S.D. Burman
With: Rishi Kapoor, Shoma Anand

Bhanwar
Dir: Bhappie Sonie
Music: R.D. Burman
With: Randhir Kapoor, Parveen Babi

Ek Se Badhkar Ek
Dir: Brij
Music: Kalyanji Anandji
With: Raaj Kumar, Navin Nischal, Sharmila Tagore

Harfan Maula
Dir: S.M. Sagar
Music: Shyamji Ghanshyamji
With: Kabir Bedi, Asha Sachdev

Mazdoor Zindabad
Dir: Naresh Kumar
Music: Usha Khanna
With: Rajendra Kumar, Mala Sinha

Rangeela Ratan
Dir: S Ramanathan
Music: Kalyanji Anandji
With: Rishi Kapoor, Parveen Babi

Shankar Dada
Dir: Shibu Mittra
Music: Sonik Omi
With: Shashi Kapoor, Neetu Singh

Santaan
Dir: Mohan Segal
Music: Laxmikant Pyarelal
With: Jeetendra, Rekha

1977
Anand Ashram
Dir: Shakti Samanta
Music: Shyamal Mittra
With: Uttam Kumar, Sharmila Tagore

Anurodh
Dir: Shakti Samanta
Music: Laxmikant Pyarelal
With: Rajesh Khanna, Simple Kapadia

Chala Murari Hero Banne
Dir: Asrani
Music: R.D. Burman
As Guest Artiste
With: Asrani, Bindiya Goswami

Dream Girl
Dir: Pramod Chakravarthy
Music: Laxmikant Pyarelal
With: Dharmendra, Hema Malini

Hira Aur Patthar
Dir: Vijay Bhatt
Music: Kalyanji Anandji
With: Shashi Kapoor, Shabana Azmi

Jadu Tona
Dir: Ravikant Nagaich
Music: Hemant Bhosale
With: Feroz Khan, Reena Roy

Khatta Meetha
Dir: Basu Chatterjee
Music: Rajesh Roshan
With: Rakesh Roshan, Bindiya Goswami

Mastan Dada
Dir: Satyen Bose
Music: Laxmikant Pyarelal
With: Sanjay Khan, Parveen Babi

Prayschit
Dir: Kamal Majumdar
Music: Laxmikant Pyarelal
With: Nanda, Parikshit Sahni

Safed Jhooth
Dir: Basu Chatterjee
Music: Shyamal Mittra
With: Vinod Mehra, Mithu Mukherjee

1978

Anmol Tasveer
Dir: Satyen Bose
Music: Vijay Raghav Rao
As Guest Artiste
With: Preeti Ganguly, Anoop Kumar

Anpadh
Dir: S.M. Sagar
Music: Hemant Bhosale
With: Sarika, Parikshit Sahni, Zarina Wahab

Apna Kanoon
Dir: B. Subhash
Music: Sonik Omi
With: Shashi Kapoor, Hema Malini

Chor Ke Ghar Chor
Dir: Vijay Sadanah
Music: Kalyanji Anandji
With: Pran, Randhir Kapoor, Zeenat Aman

Dil Aur Deewar
Dir: K. Bapaiah
Music: Laxmikant Pyarelal
With: Nirupa Roy, Jeetendra, Rakesh Roshan, Moushumi Chatterjee

Do Musafir
Dir: Devendra Goel
Music: Kalyanji Anandji
With: Pran, Rekha, Shashi Kapoor

Mehfil
Dir: Amar Kumar
Music: Shankar Jaikishen
With: Sadhana, Anil Dhawan

Phool Khile Hain Gulshan Gulshan
Dir: Sikander Khanna
Music: Laxmikant Pyarelal
With: Rishi Kapoor, Moushumi Chatterjee

Tumhare Liye
Dir: Basu Chatterjee
Music: Jaidev
With: Sanjeev Kumar, Vidya Sinha

1979
Bagula Bhagat
Dir: Harmesh Malhotra
Music: Kalyanji Anandji
With: Shatrughan Sinha, Shabana Azmi

Guru Ho Ja Shuru
Dir: Shiv Kumar
Music: Kalyanji Anandji
With: Mahendra Sandhu, Prema Narayan

Janata Hawaldar
Dir: Mehmood
Music: Rajesh Roshan
With: Rajesh Khanna, Hema Malini, Yogeeta Bali, Mehmood

1980
Aakhri Insaf
Dir: Kalidas
Music: Rajesh Roshan
With: Zarina Wahab, Vijayendra

Aap Ke Deewane
Dir: Surendra Mohan
Music: Rajesh Roshan
With: Rishi Kapoor, Rakesh Roshan, Tina Munim

Judaai
Dir: T. Rama Rao
Music: Laxmikant Pyarelal
With: Jeetendra, Rekha

Khubsoorat
Dir: Hrishikesh Mukherjee
Music: R.D. Burman
With: Rekha, Rakesh Roshan

Nazrana Pyar Ka
Dir: S.M. Sagar
Music: Hemant Bhosale
With: Sarika, Vijayendra

Sau Din Saas Ke
Dir: Vijay Sadanah
Music: Kalyanji Anandji
With: Asha Parekh, Reena Roy, Raj Babbar

Saajan Mere Main Saajan Ki
Dir: Hiren Nag
Music: Ravindra Jain
With: Raj Kiran, Rameshwari

Takkar
Dir: K. Bapaiah
Music: R.D. Burman
With: Jeetendra, Zeenat Aman

Shaukeen
Dir: Basu Chatterjee
Music: R.D. Burman
With: Mithun Chakravarthy, Rati Agnihotri

Sumbandh
Dir: Shibu Mittra
Music: Bappi Lahiri
With: Vinod Mehra, Rati Agnihotri

1981

Chalti Ka Naam Zindagi
Dir: Kishore Kumar
Music: Kishore Kumar
With: Kishore Kumar, Anoop Kumar, Amit Kumar, Reeta Bhaduri, Y Vijaya

Jyoti
Dir: Pramod Chakravarthy
Music: Bappi Lahiri
With: Jeetendra, Hema Malini

Jail Yatra
Dir: Bhappi Sonie
Music: R.D. Burman
With: Vinod Khanna, Reena Roy

Maan Gaye Ustad
Dir: Shibu Kumar
Music: Sonik Omi
With: Shashi Kapoor, Hema Malini

Yeh Kaisa Nasha Hai
Dir: D.S. Sultania
Music: Chand Pardesi
With: Dr Shreeram Lagoo, Deven Varma

1982

Anokha Bandhan
Dir: Mehul Kumar
Music: Usha Khanna
With: Shabana Azmi, Navin Nischal

Chor Mandli
Dir: C.L. Rawal
Music: Kalyanji Anandji
With: Raj Kapoor, Asha Parekh

Chor Police
Dir: Amjad Khan
Music: R.D. Burman
With: Shatrughan Sinha, Parveen Babi

Dial 100
Dir: S. Ramanathan
Music: Bappi Lahiri
With: Vinod Mehra, Bindiya Goswami

Dushmanee
Dir: Dinesh Saxena
Music: Laxmikant Pyarelal
With: Shatrughan Sinha, Moushumi Chatterjee

Ek Daku Shaher Mein
Dir: Kalidas
Music: Rajesh Roshan
With: Sarika, Suresh Oberoi

Haadsa
Dir: Akbar Khan
Music: Kalyanji Anandji
With: Smita Patil, Akbar Khan, Ranjeeta

Heeron Ka Chor
Dir: S.K. Kapur
Music: Sonik Omi
With: Mithun Chakravarthy, Bindiya Goswami, Madan Puri

Love in Goa
Dir: Hersh Kohli
Music: Bappi Lahiri
With: Anuradha, Mayur

Mehandi Rang Laayegi
Dir: Dasari Narayan Rao
Music: Laxmikant Pyarelal
With: Jeetendra, Rekha

Patthar Ki Lakeer
Dir: Din Dayal Sharma
Music: Usha Khanna
With: Sarika, Deepak Parashar

Phir Aayee Barsaat
Dir: Jaiprakash
Music: Kuldeep Singh
As Guest Artiste
With: Anuradha, Sunil Lahiri

1983
Bekaraar
Dir: V.B. Rajendra Prasad
Music:
With: Sanjay Dutt, Mohnish Behl, Padmini Kolhapure

Mahaan
Dir: S. Ramanathan
Music: R.D. Burman
With: Amitabh Bachchan, Waheeda Rehman

1984
Akalmand
Dir: Raj Bharath
Music: Laxmikant Pyarelal
With: Jeetendra, Sri Devi

Duniya
Dir: Ramesh Talwar
Music: R.D. Burman
With: Dilip Kumar, Rishi Kapoor, Amrita Singh

Farishta
Dir: Sunil Sikand
Music: R.D. Burman
With: Kamaljeet, Smita Patil

Raja Aur Rana
Dir: Shibu Mittra
Music: Bappi Lahiri
With: Pran, Punit Issar

1985
Bhago Bhoot Aaya
Dir: Krishna Naidu
Music: Hemant Bhosale
With: Deven Varma, Kaajal Kiran

Grahasti
Dir: Prashant Nanda
Music: Ravindra Jain
With: Suresh Oberoi, Yogeeta Bali

Durga
Dir: Shibu Mitra
Music: Sonik Omi
With: Hema Malini, Raj Babbar, Pran

Farz Ki Keemat
Dir: Sudhir Wahi
Music: Sonik Omi
With: Premnath, Satish Kaul, Bhavana Bhatt

Tawaif
Dir: B.R. Chopra
Music: Ravi
With: Rishi Kapoor, Poonam Dhillon

1984–85
Hum Log
Commentary for TV serial
Dir: Kumar Vasudev

1986
Amma
Dir: Jiten
Music: Rajkamal
With: Raakhee, Mithun Chakravarthy

Inteqam Ki Aag
Dir: Shiv Kumar
Music: Shankar Jaikishen
With: Zarina Wahab, Mahendra Sandhu

Pyar Kiya Hai Pyar Karenge
Dir: Vijay Reddy
Music: Laxmikant Pyarelal
With: Anil Kapoor, Padmini Kolhapure

Ram Tera Desh
Dir: Swaroop Kumar
Music: Annu Malik
With: Hema Malini, Vijayendra

Shatru
Dir: Pramod Chakravarthy
Music: R.D. Burman
With: Rajesh Khanna, Shabana Siddique

1987
Awaam
Dir: B.R. Chopra
Music: Ravi
With: Rajesh Khanna, Raj Babbar, Smita Patil, Poonam Dhillon

Hifazat
Dir: Prayag Raj
Music: R.D. Burman
With: Anil Kapoor, Nutan, Madhuri Dixit

Mr India
Dir: Shekhar Kapoor
Music: Laxmikant Pyarelal
With: Anil Kapoor, Sridevi

Watan Ke Rakhwale
Dir: T. Rama Rao
Music: Laxmikant Pyarelal
With: Sunil Dutt, Sridevi, Dharmendra, Moushumi Chatterjee, Mithun Chakravarty

Woh Din Aayega
Dir: Satyen Bose
Music: Alok Ganguly
With: Raj Kiran, Rajan Sippy, Divya Rana

1986-87
Dada Dadi Ki Kahani
TV Serial
Dir: Moti Sagar

1988
Clerk
Dir: Manoj Kumar
Music: Uttam Jagdish
With: Manoj Kumar, Rajendra Kumar, Rekha

Bahadur Shah Zafar
TV Serial
Dir: B.R. Chopra, Ravi Chopra

1989
Bhim Bhavani
TV Serial
Dir: Basu Chatterjee

(Publisher's Note: This select filmography, as compiled by Nabendu Ghosh in 1995, lists all of Ashok Kumar's significant appearances in cinema and on television. Therefore, it has not been updated for this new edition. Ashok Kumar accepted very few roles after 1989, appearing in some twenty films, including Return of the Jewel Thief *(1996)*. His last film role was in the Bengali film Achena Atithi, released in 1997.)

Ashok Kumar in some of his earliest movies.

Izzat (1937), Ashok Kumar's fourth film with Devika Rani.

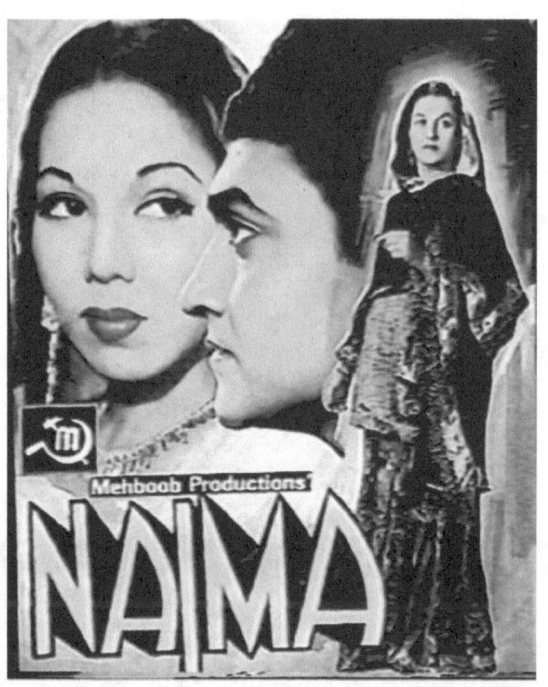

Najma (1943), the first Muslim social which also made Ashok Kumar a superstar.

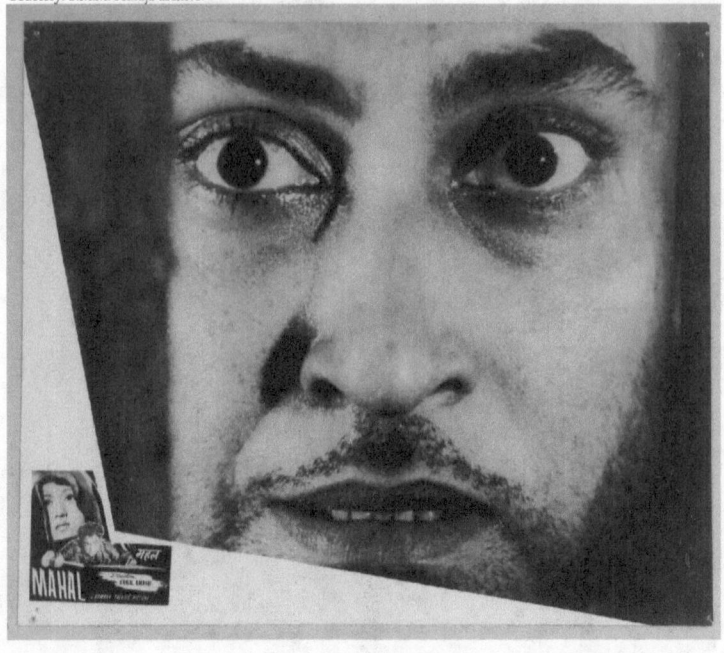

Mahal (1949).

Ziddi (1948).

Parineeta (1953).

Ashok Kumar, Meena Kumari, Protima Devi in *Parineeta* (1953).

The brothers, Ashok, Anoop and Kishore Kumar, in *Chalti Ka Naam Gaadi* (1958).
Courtesy: S.M.M. Ausaja archive.

Ashok Kumar with Rita Bahaduri in *Chalti Ka Naam Zindagi* (1981), the last of the triology starring the three brothers.

The final confrontation between Ashok Kumar and Nutan in *Bandini* (1963).

A still from *Jewel Thief* (1967).

A still from *Aashirwad* (1963), for which he won the National Award for Best Actor.

Courtesy: S.M.M. Ausaja archive.

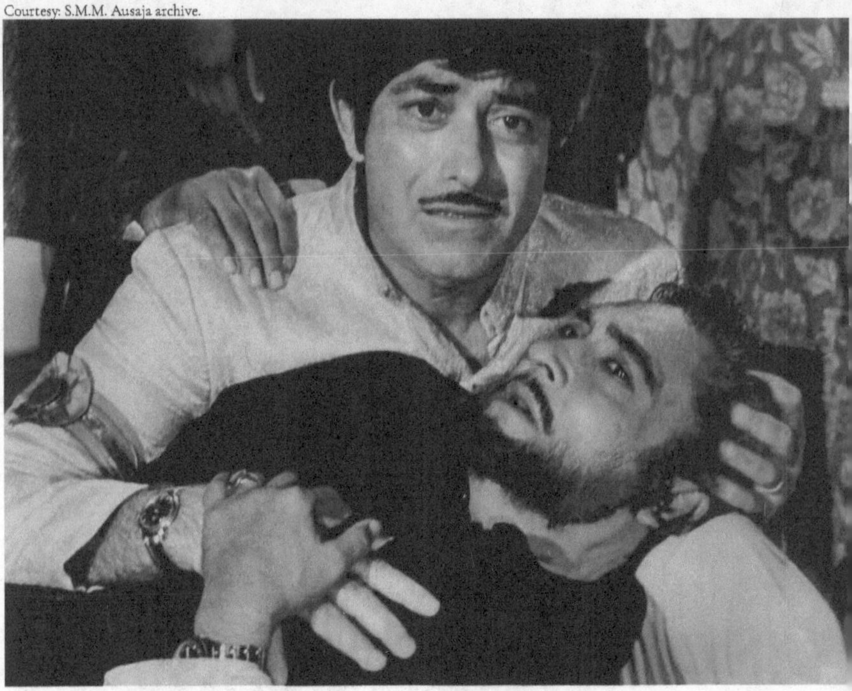

With Raaj Kumar in a still from *Pakeezah* (1971).

Ashok Kumar and Helen in *Aansoo Ban Gaye Phool* (1969).

Courtesy: S.M.M. Ausaja archive.

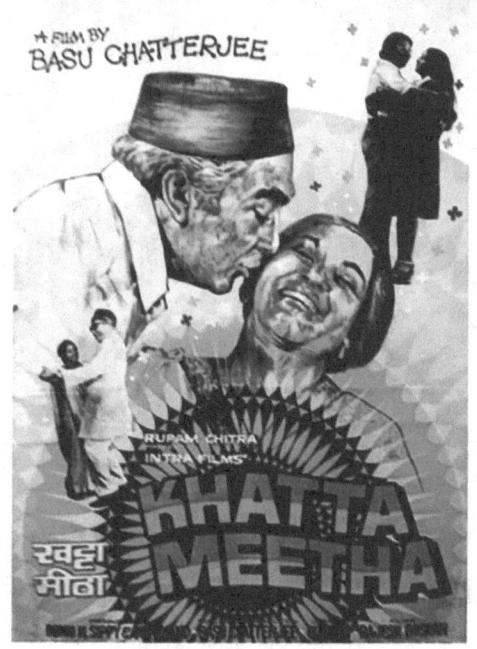

Khatta Meetha (1977).

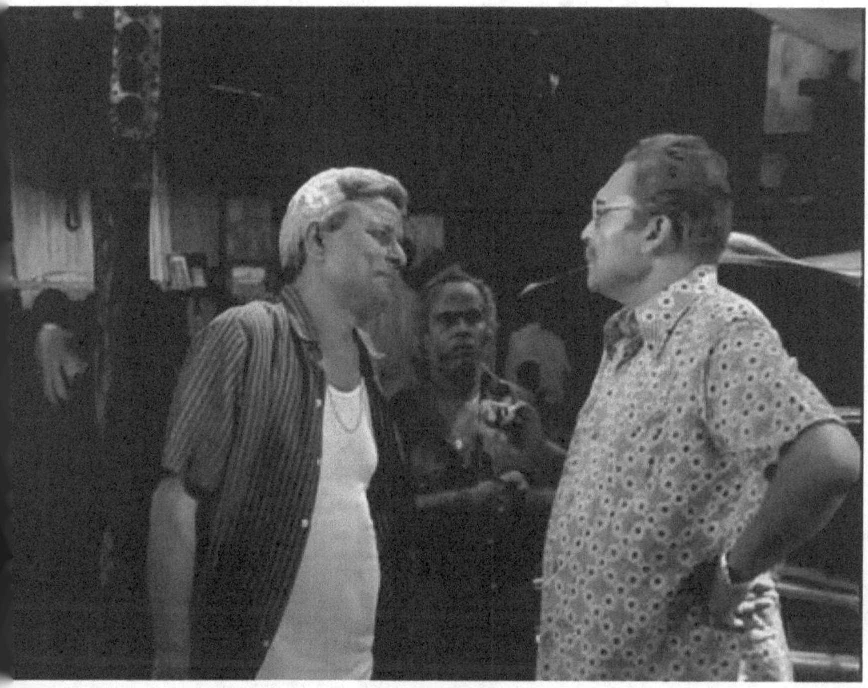

A still from the superhit *Chhoti Si Baat* (1975).

A still from *Aap Beetee* (1976).

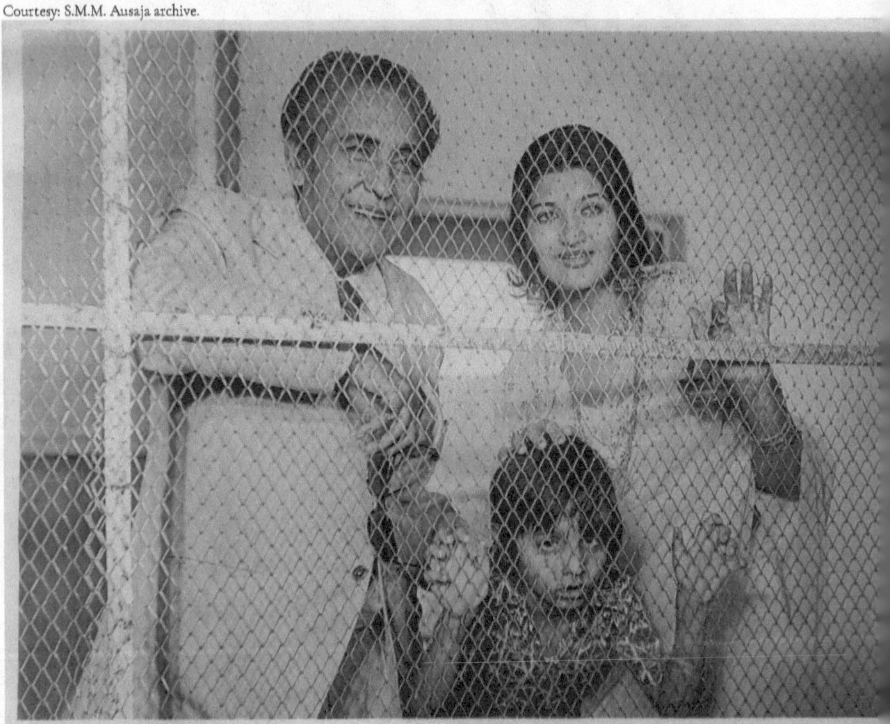

A still from *Anpadh* (1978).

On the cover of the 1961 issue of *Filmfare*.

The first film actor to appear in advertisements.

The statue of Himanshu Rai, founder of Bombay Talkies, which was found discarded after Devika Rani took over Bombay Talkies after his death.

S.M.M. Ausaja archive.

The superhits produced by Bombay Talkies.

Former president R. Venkataraman felicitating Ashok Kumar with the Dadasaheb Phalke award in 1989.

A self-portrait by the actor.

Kunjalal Ganguly and Gouri Rani Devi, Ashok Kumar's parents.

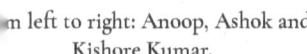

From left to right: Anoop, Ashok and Kishore Kumar.

Ashok Kumar with his wife, Shobha.

Index

Aag, 75
Aansoo Ban Gaye Phool, xxiv, 82, 129, 162
Aarti, xii, 84, 156
Aashirwad, xiv, 86, 87, 102, 105, 125, 126, 162
Abbas, Khwaja Ahmed, 27, 51
Abhimaan, 13
Academy of Dramatic Arts, 26
Acharya, N.R., 50, 51, 79, 143, 144
Achhut Kanya, xiii, xv, xxii, 44, 45, 46, 47, 49, 102, 124, 125, 142
Adampur Dramatic Club, 12, 13, 16
Afsana 74, 75, 83, 107, 126, 147, 160
Ajmeri, Nazir, 59
Akash Deep, 84
Alibaba Chalis Chor, 55
Aman, Zeenat, 83, 167, 169, 173, 176
Amrohi, Kamal, 59, 64, 79, 126, 146, 165
Anand Aashram, 85
Angoothi, 55, 144
Anjaan, 51, 144
Anjangarh, 6600
Anurupa Devi, 16
Anuraag, 85, 165
Arjun Pandit, 87, 170
Ashok Kumar iii, v, vii, x, xii, xv, xix, xx, xxi, xxii, xxiii, xxiv, xxv, 3, 4, 5, 6, 7, 9, 10, 12, 13, 15, 16, 19, 20–25, 27, 40, 43, 46, 49, 50–62, 65–68, 70, 71, 73, 74–76, 78–89, 91–95, 97, 99, 101–113, 117, 120–130, 132–141 *see* Ganguly, Ashok Kumar
Ashrunchi Jhali Phoole, 82
Atithi, 80
Azad, 50, 143

Baadbaan, xxiv, 79, 84, 150
Bachchan, Amitabh, 105, 169, 179
Bahadur Shah Zafar, 87, 138, 183
Bali, Geeta, 83, 110, 111, 147, 148, 151, 154
Bali, Vyjayantimala, 81, 110, 126, 153, 159, 160, 161
Banaphool, 12, 80
Bandhan, 50, 51, 55, 106, 144, 177

Bandi, 82, 151
Bandini, xii, xxiv, 76, 78, 89, 126, 158
Bandish, 81, 82, 150
Banerjee, Ajitesh, 81
Banerjee, Durgadas, 25
Banerjee, Satish Chandra, 10, 11, 24
Banerjee, Shibchandra, 7, 8, 9, 10, 12, 15
Baran, Timir, 79, 150
Barsaat, 75, 179
Ben, Hur, 52
Benazir, 78, 159
Betaab, 75, 148
Bewafa, 75, 148
Bhaduri, Sisir, 25, 37, 66
Bhagalpur, vii, 7, 8, 11, 12, 113, 114, 117, 133
Bhai, Behen, 84
Bhai Bhai, xvi, 110, 151
Bhanumati, 110, 149
Bharat Bhushan, xxiv, 66, 159, 160
Bharat Muni, 99
Bhim Bhavani, 87, 183
Bhim Singh, A., 84, 159, 161, 162, 166
Bhuvan Shome, 12, 80
Bilva Mangal, 12
Bombay Talkies, vi, viii, xxii, xxiii, xxiv, 3, 13, 16, 24, 25, 27, 28, 31, 33, 35, 36, 46, 48, 49, 50, 52, 54, 55, 56, 57, 58, 59, 65, 68, 69, 70, 75, 79, 82, 88, 99, 106, 114, 124, 125, 128, 129, 134, 136, 139, 141

Bombay Talkies Workers Cooperative Society, 79
Bose, Devaki, 25, 56, 80
Bose, Nitin, 65, 75, 79, 126, 147, 159, 165
Bose, Satyen, xxiv, 81, 82, 126, 132, 150–153, 155, 162, 166, 172, 173, 182
Bose, Tarun, 78
Brij, 83, 154, 158, 160, 163, 166, 168, 169, 170
Burman, Sachin Dev, 56, 65, 78, 82, 145, 146, 147, 152, 153, 158, 159, 161, 164–170

Chakravarty, Amiya, 27, 51, 53, 54, 128, 144
Chal Chal Re Naujawan, 55, 56, 128, 145
Chalti Ka Naam Gaadi, 82, 126, 132, 152
Champ, The, 52
Chanderi Duniyet, 50
Chandidas, 25, 66, 80
Chandraprabha, 55, 144
Chandrasekhar, 56, 80
Chatterjee, Bankim Chandra, 7, 80
Chatterjee, Basu, 83, 87, 107, 120, 130, 172, 174, 176, 183
Chatterjee, Sarat Chandra, xx, 15, 16
Chattopadhyay, Harindranath, 86
Chaudhuri Col. M.N., 26
Chowdhury, Salil, xi, 83, 169
Chheley Kaar, 81
Chhoti Si Baat, 83, 126, 169

184 INDEX

Chitnis, Leela, xxiv, 49, 50, 51, 110, 126, 143–145
Chitralekha, 84, 126, 159
Chopra, Baldev Raj, xi, 73, 74, 75, 79, 83, 87, 99, 100, 102, 105, 126, 138, 147, 149, 151, 155, 158, 167, 180, 181, 183
Chopra, Ravi, 87, 183
Chori Mera Kaam, 83, 169
Colman, Ronald, 92
Chughtai, Ismat, 59, 60, 126
Chunilal, Rai Bahadur, 54, 55

Deedar, 75, 147
Dev Anand, viii, xiii, 27, 60, 61, 66, 75, 79, 84, 105, 127, 149, 150, 161
Devika Rani, xxii, 26, 27, 31, 37, 38, 39, 40, 41, 44, 46, 48, 49, 50, 51, 53–57, 100, 110, 125, 126, 128, 136, 142–144
Dharmendra, xii, 78, 158, 159, 160, 161, 163, 164, 169, 172, 182
Dilip Kumar *see* Yusuf Khan
Dixit, Madhuri, 105, 182
Doctor, 66, 85
Do Bhai, xii, 83, 163
Do Bigha Zameen, 85
Durgacharan, 7
Dutt, Nargis, 75, 110, 126, 145, 146, 147, 148
Dutt, Sunil, xiii, 74, 75, 99, 151, 157, 158, 161, 162, 166, 167, 182

Eight Days, 56, 145

Ek Doctor ki Maut, 80
Ek Hi Rasta, 74, 151

Fideltronic Sound System, 36
Filmistan, 55, 56, 57, 65, 125, 128

Gandhi, Indira, 9, 46
Gandhi, Mohandas Karamchand, 20
Gangopadhyay, Upendranath, 12
Ganguly, Anoop Kumar, 121, 131, 152, 173, 176
Ganguly, Anoop, 94, 95, 120, 130, 131
Ganguly, Ashok Kumar Acting Style, 3, 40, 99, 124
 Astrologist, The, 89
 Awards, 89, 90, 93, 101, 107, 113, 127
 Birth, xxiii, 132
 Businessman, The, 108
 Chess Player, The, 88
 Childhood, The, 13, 67, 73, 138
 Education, 23, 133
 Homeopath, The, 94
 Limericist, The, 94
 Linguist, The, 92
 Lover of Vintage Cars, 91
 Marriage, 24
 Painter, The, 91
 Singer, The, 94
Ganguly, Gouri Rani Devi (Banerjee), 7, 10
Ganguly, Kalyan *see* Ganguly Anoop Kumar Ganguly, Kishore Kumar,

INDEX 185

Ganguly, Kumud Kumar *see* Ganguly Ashok Kumar
Ganguly, Kunjalal,
Ganguly, Preeti, xix, 130, 138, 173
Ganguly, Shobha (Bandopadhyaya), 9, 62, 90, 99–100, 109, 117–122, 130
Ghosh, Dani, 25
Ghosh, Girish Chandra, 12
Gumrah, 158
Gupta, Dinen, 81

Haatey Bajarey, 80, 81, 106, 126
Haider, Ghulam, 59, 145, 146
Hardinge Hostel, 24
Harley, 27
Hasrat Lucknowi, 59
Hemant Kumar, 79, 150, 151
Hospital, xvi, xix, 80, 126, 155
Howard, Leslie, 48
Howrah Bridge, 85, 126, 132, 134, 153
Hum Log, 87, 127, 138, 180
Humayun, 56, 128, 139, 145
Humrahi, 66
Hussein, Najmul, 3, 31, 32

Iftikhar, xvi, 88, 91, 93
Inspector, x, 41, 42, 62, 84, 134, 151
Inteqam, 109, 163, 181
Irani, Daisy, 81, 150
Iswar Chandra Vidyasagar, 9
Izzat, 49, 142

Jalpari, 75, 148

Janma Bhoomi, 49, 142
Jaywant, Nalini, 65, 67, 79, 110, 111, 126, 130, 147–149, 150, 152
Jeejeebhoy House, 63, 64
Jeetendra, 83, 163, 164, 168, 171, 173, 175, 176, 178, 179
Jeevan Naiya, viii, xxv, 18, 31, 36, 42, 43, 44, 45, 49, 105, 112, 114, 124, 136, 142
Jewel Thief, 84, 125, 161
Jhoola, xiii, 51, 106, 144
Joglekar, Vasant, 88, 150, 153, 155, 157, 162
Johar, I.S., 73

Kabuliwala, 80
Kafila, xxiv, 75, 103, 148
Kalpana, 79, 109, 155
Kamini Kaushal, 60, 110, 148, 153
Kanan Devi, 56, 80, 88, 110, 117, 126, 146
Kanetkar, Vasant, 82
Kangan, 49, 50, 51, 106, 143, 154, 165
Kanoon, x, xi, 74, 75, 126, 155, 160, 173
Kapal Kundala, 66
Kapoor, Anil, 105, 181, 182
Kapoor, Raj, xvii, 75, 105, 127, 138, 148, 177
Kapoor, Shashi, 67, 83, 157, 159, 169, 170–173, 177
Karma, 19, 27, 123, 139
Karnarjun, 114

Kaur, Kuldip, 73
Khalil, S., 78, 159
Khandwa, vii, 9, 10, 11, 20, 21, 22, 23, 25, 47, 114, 115
Khatta Meetha, xiv, 83, 84, 126, 130, 172
Khemchand Prakash, 65, 146, 149
Khubsoorat, 87, 106, 175
Khursheed, xvi, 122
Kishore Kumar *see* Ganguly, Kishore Kumar viii, xviii, 23, 61, 65, 82, 90, 101, 121, 127, 129, 131, 135, 151–153, 164, 166, 176
Kismet, v, xxii, 48, 52–55, 66, 94, 106, 125, 144
Koro, 109
Kshudhita Pashan, 80

Laughton, Charles, 48, 92
Light of Asia, 26

Maa, xxiv, 66, 69, 95, 115, 116, 133, 161, 164
Mackesti, William Desmond, 25
Madhubala, ix, 65, 82, 85, 110, 111, 126, 129, 132–134, 146, 147, 151, 152, 153
Madhurika, 49, 143
Mahajan, K.K., 83
Mahal, ix, xx, 65, 69, 125, 126, 132, 146, 169
Majboor, viii, 59, 60, 69
Malik, 84, 181
Mallik, Amar, 100
Malone, Rajendra, 73

Mamta, 84, 126, 161, 164
Mangeshkar, Lata, ix, 65
Manto, Sadat Hasan, 59, 60, 89, 102
Mantra Shakti, 16
Marion, Francis, 52, 53
Mashal, viii, 65, 69, 147
Mastan Dada, 82, 172
Masoom, 82, 155
Massey, 39, 40, 41
Maya Devi, 49, 110, 143
Mazumdar, Phani, xxiv, 65, 79, 84, 85, 106
Mazumdar, Sushil, 80, 100, 145, 155
Meena Bazaar, 59, 89, 102
Meena Kumari, 66, 74, 76, 79, 81, 110, 111, 126, 149, 150, 151, 152, 153, 156, 159, 160, 164, 165
Mehboob Khan, 55, 126, 128, 139
Meherban, 84, 161
Meri Soorat Teri Aankhen, xi, 79
Mili, xiv, 87, 105, 169
Mitra B., 55
Mitra, Gajendra Kumar, 49
Mukherjee, Aparesh, 114
Mukherjee, Arun Kumar, 13, 133
Mukherjee, Gyan, xxiv, 24, 48, 51–55, 66–68, 79, 144, 145, 147, 149, 150, 151
Mukherjee, Hrishikesh, xxiv, 85, 87, 105, 126, 162, 163, 169, 170, 175
Mukherjee, Indu, 114
Mukherjee, Sashadhar, viii, 3, 23,

24, 27, 49, 50, 53, 55, 58, 119, 128
Mukherjee, Sati Rani (Ganguly), 23, 24, 58, 119
Mumtaz Ali, 27
Mumtaz Shanti, 53, 110, 144, 146
Munawar Sultan, 59
Muqaddar, 65, 69

Naaz, 78, 111, 150
Nai Rahen, 83, 154
Naidu, Sarojini, 46
Najma, xxiii, 55, 128, 145
Nanda, 74, 126, 155, 157, 160, 163, 165, 172, 180
Narayani, 50
Naseem, 110, 145, 148
Natya Shastra, 99
Nau Bahar, 75, 148
Navin Nischal, 165, 166, 168, 170, 177
Naya Sansar, 51, 54, 144
Nayyar, O.P., 85, 152, 153, 155, 157, 162, 167
Nazim Panipati, 59
Nehru, Jawaharlal, 46
New Theatres, xxiv, 15, 16, 25, 55, 65, 66, 85, 100
Niranjan Pal, 34
Nirmala, 49, 143
Nutan, xii, 78, 110, 111, 126, 129, 153, 158, 161, 162, 164, 182

Ojha, S.K., 79, 146, 150
Oonchey Log, xii, 84, 126, 160
Osten, Franz, viii, xxii, 27, 29, 30, 32, 37, 39, 42, 44, 45, 46, 49, 50, 79, 142, 143

Pabst, 26
Padamsee, Pearl, 84, 159
Padmini, 83, 109, 110, 146, 153, 155, 160, 179, 181
Pahela Aadmi, 66
Pai, Dattaram, 145
Paise Ki Gudiya, 83, 168
Pal, S.K., 150
Palekar, Amol, 83, 169
Palsikar, Nana, 27
Palu, xix, 93, 94, 95, 96, 97, 120, 131 *See* Ganguly, Preeti
Parineeta, xx, xxiv, 13, 75, 76, 126, 129, 133, 149
Patel, Anuradha, 120, 130
Patel, Baburao, 111
Patel, Bharati (Ganguly), 120, 131, 165
Polo, Eddie, 25
Pooja Ke Phool, 84, 159
Poonam, 75, 148, 180, 181
Pradeep Kumar, 83, 156, 157, 158, 159, 160
Pradhan, Snehprabha, 27
Pran, 73, 83, 107, 164, 166, 173, 180
Prem Kahani, 49, 143
Puran Bhagat, 25, 80

Raag Rang, 75, 148
Raagini, 79
Raakhi, xii, 84, 166
Rachebean, Andre, 36
Raghunath, 5, 169

Rai, Bina, 74, 110, 149, 150, 151, 152, 161
Rai, Himanshu, viii, xxii, 3, 26–30, 32, 34–38, 42–44, 46, 47, 48, 50, 53, 57, 61, 62, 66, 67, 70, 82, 112, 120, 124, 129
Rajanigandha, 49
Rajendra Kumar, 3, 74, 154, 155, 158, 170, 182
Rajendra Prasad, 24, 101, 179
Rathaoni, Akos, 56
Rehana Sultan, 167
Rehman, Waheeda, xii, 84, 126, 157, 167, 179
Reinhardt, Max, 26
Rekha, 87, 105, 126, 166, 168, 169, 171, 173, 175, 178, 182
Renuka Devi, 51, 110, 144
Roerich, Devika Rani *See* Devika Rani
Roerich, Svetoslav, 56, 136
Rogho *see* Raghunath
Roopsri Studio, 89
Roy, Bimal, xxiii, xxiv, 13, 66, 75, 76, 78, 79, 81, 85, 126, 137, 149, 158
Roy, D.L., 12
Roy, Hemendralal, 12
Roy, Jyotirmoy, 81
Roy, Nirupa, 110, 151, 153, 154, 155, 156, 158, 160, 173
Royal Academy of Music, 26
Ruma Devi, 65, 147

Sa-Re-Ga-Ma-Pa, 82, 166
Sadhana, 109, 158, 163, 166, 174
Safar, 84, 164
Safed Jhooth, 84, 172
Sagar Sangamey, 80
Sagina Mahato, 80
Saha, Meghnad, 24
Sahu, Kishore, 27, 146, 158
Saigal, Kundanlal, 55
Saira Banu, 83, 126, 161, 164, 166, 168
Samanta, Shakti, 84, 106, 126, 134, 151, 152, 153, 165, 171
Saloni, 75, 149
Samar, 16, 65
Sangram, ix, 48, 67, 68, 69, 136, 147
Sapera, 66
Saraswati Devi, 34, 142, 143, 144
Sarkar, Birendra, 15
Satyakam, 87, 163
Savera, 82, 126, 153
Savitri, 49, 143
School for Scandal, 83
Sen, Arvind, 148
Sen, Asit, xxiv, 84, 161, 164
Sen, Suchitra, 80, 110, 111, 126, 155, 161
Shah, Shantilal, 94
Shahid Latif, 59, 60, 61
Shakila, 83, 156, 157, 158
Sharafat, xxiv, 84, 164
Sharma, Kidar, 84
Shaukeen, 84, 125, 126, 136, 176
Sheroo, 84, 152
Shesh Saptak, 5
Shikari, 56, 65, 146
Shiraz, 26
Sholay, 54, 74
Shukla, Ravi Shankar, 41, 42

Shyam, 59, 113, 114, 116–119
Shyama, xxiv, 66, 110, 147, 154, 155, 157
Sinha, Mala, 75, 83, 99, 110, 126, 154, 158, 159, 160, 161, 163, 165, 170
Sinha, Tapan, 80, 81, 134, 167
Sinha, Vidya, 83, 169, 174
Sitaron Se Aagey, 82
Spratti, Count Von, 36
Street Singer, 66
Sumitra Devi, 65, 110, 147
Suraiya, 27, 110, 147

Tabassum, 68
Tagore, Rabindranath, xxii, 5, 26
Tagore, Sharmila, 85, 126, 162, 163, 164, 166, 169, 170, 171
Tale of Two Cities, A, 47
Tamasha, 65, 66, 69, 75, 111, 149
Tara Sundari, 25
Three Headed Cobra, The, 56
Thief of Baghdad, 55
Throw of Dice, A, 26
Tracy, Spencer, 48

Tumhare Liye, 84, 174

Uday Shankar Ballet Group, 79
Udayer Pathey, 66, 81
Usha Kiron, 152
Ustadon ke Ustad, 83, 158
Uttam Kumar, 4, 85, 106, 171

Vacha, Savak, 31, 36, 56, 58
Vachan, 49, 114, 118, 143
Veena, 73, 82, 110, 145, 147, 150, 152, 165
Verma, Deven, 120, 130
Verma, Roopa (Ganguly), 120
Victoria No. 203, 203 83, 107, 126, 136
Vidyapati, 80
Vijay Anand, xiii, 84, 126, 138, 161

Wirsching, Carl Josef, 27

Yusuf Khan, xvii, 3, 27, 75, 105, 126, 127, 129, 147, 179

Ziddi, viii, 61, 69, 127, 129